# The Anatomy and Physiology
of Obstetrics

*Other books by the late Mr C. W. F. Burnett*
*and revised by Miss M. Anderson*

A Summary of Gynaecology

# The Anatomy and Physiology of Obstetrics

*A Short Textbook for Students and Midwives*

*by the late* C. W. F. BURNETT, MD, FRCS, FRCOG

Revised by
MARY M. ANDERSON, MB, ChB, FRCOG

*Consultant Obstetrician and Gynaecologist,
Lewisham Hospital, London*

Wolfe Publishing Ltd

Published by
Wolfe Publishing Ltd
Brook House
2–16 Torrington Place
London WC1E 7LT

Reprinted 1992, by Richard Clay Ltd., Bungay, Suffolk

First published in 1953 by Faber and Faber Limited. Second edition 1959. Third edition 1962. Fourth edition 1965, reprinted 1966. Fifth edition 1969, reprinted 1971, 1972. Sixth edition 1979, reprint 1981, 1984 (with amendments), 1987, 1989.

ISBN 0 7234 1835 7

For full details of all Wolfe titles please write to Wolfe Publishing Ltd, Brook House, 2–16 Torrington Place, London WC1E 7LT, England.

*British Library Cataloging in Publication Data*
Burnett, Clifford William Furneaux
The anatomy and physiology of obstetrics – 6th ed.
1. Generative organs, Female
2. Women – Physiology
I. Title    II. Anderson, Mary M
612.6'2        QP259
ISBN 0 7234 1835 7

# Contents

## Preface to the Sixth Edition

Basic anatomy and physiology never changes and Mr. Burnett's teaching remains as clear and concise as ever. A few of the older anatomical terms have been altered or omitted and new physiological facts introduced. I am indebted to Mrs. Anne Barrett for re-illustrating the book.

It has been a privilege to revise this work originally written by such a distinguished teacher of midwives.

*M.M.A. 1979*

# Illustrations

*Chapter One*

# The Anatomy of the Female Genital Organs

The female genital organs are made up of the external genitalia, which comprise the structures of the vulva, and the internal genitalia, which include the vagina, uterus, Fallopian tubes and ovaries. These may together be said to form the female genital tract.

## THE VULVA

The vulva (Fig. 1/1) is formed from the following structures:

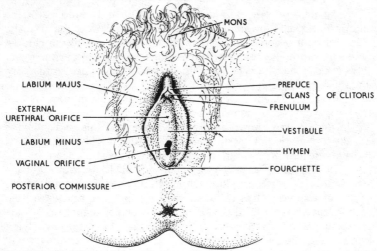

**Fig. 1/1:** The Vulva

1. The mons veneris is a pad of fatty tissue situated in front of the symphysis pubis, covered by skin and pubic hairs which develop at the time of puberty. The hair is short and of the same colour as the hair

of the scalp, with a typical distribution extending about one-third of the distance up to the umbilicus. Occasionally it reaches as high as this structure and then has the distribution which occurs normally in the male.

2. The labia majora (each of which is known in the singular as a labium majus) consist of two rounded folds of fatty tissue and skin, which extend downwards and backwards from the mons veneris, enclosing between them the urogenital cleft. As they pass towards the anus they become flatter and merge into the perineal body, which lies between the lower end of the vagina in front and the anal canal behind. Their outer surface is covered with short hairs after puberty, while their inner surface is smooth and contains numerous sweat and sebaceous glands. The terminal portions of the round ligaments of the uterus end in the fatty tissues of the labia majora.

3. The labia minora (which are known in the singular as a labium minus) are two smaller folds of pink skin lying longitudinally within the encircling labia majora and enclosing between them the vestibule. They are quite smooth and devoid of hairs and fat, but they contain a few sweat and sebaceous glands and are very vascular.

When traced upwards and forwards each labium minus is seen to split into two smaller folds. The upper one of these unites with its fellow of the opposite side and forms the hood or prepuce of the clitoris; the smaller lower fold also joins with its fellow of the opposite side and both become attached to the under surface of the clitoris, where they form the frenulum of the clitoris. Thus the upper and lower folds enclose the clitoris between them, with the prepuce lying above and the frenulum below.

When traced downwards and backwards the labia minora encircle the vagina and become joined together at their posterior extremities by a thin fold of skin known as the fourchette. It is this fold which is usually torn at the time of the patient's first delivery, however expert the midwife may be in controlling the birth of the baby's head.

4. The clitoris (Fig. 1/2) is a small extremely sensitive erectile structure situated in the midline within the preputial and frenular folds of the labia minora. It is about 2.5cm long and is composed of two corpora cavernosa, which are small erectile bodies lying side by side and extending backwards to be attached on each side to the underlying bones of the pubic arch. These portions are known as the crura (crus in the singular) of the clitoris. The pointed extremity of the clitoris or glans surmounts its body and is continuous with the vestibular bulbs.

These structures are all extremely vascular with a plentiful nerve supply, and are attached by a small suspensory ligament to the front of the symphysis pubis. They correspond to similar structures which

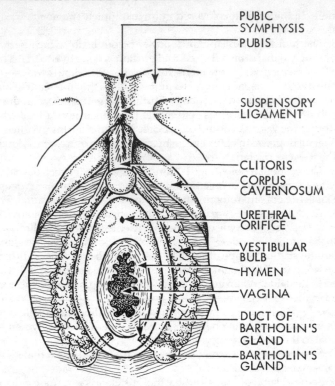

PUBIC
SYMPHYSIS
PUBIS

SUSPENSORY
LIGAMENT

CLITORIS
CORPUS
CAVERNOSUM

URETHRAL
ORIFICE

VESTIBULAR
BULB

HYMEN

VAGINA

DUCT OF
BARTHOLIN'S
GLAND

BARTHOLIN'S
GLAND

**Fig. 1/2:**    The clitoris and vestibular bulbs

form the penis of the male, but are much smaller in size and do not transmit the urethra.

5. The vestibule is the narrow cleft lying between the labia minora, which must be separated to bring it into view. It contains the openings of the urethra above and the vagina below.

6. The urethral meatus is a small opening lying about 2.5cm below the clitoris in the anterior part of the vestibule. In appearance it is a small vertical slit with slightly prominent margins. Two small dimples are usually present on each side of the orifice—these are the openings of Skene's tubules. These structures are two small blind tubules which run for about 6mm parallel to the course of the urethra within its wall.

7. The vaginal orifice is also known as the introitus vaginae and occupies the lower two-thirds of the vestibule, lying between the labia

minora. In the virgin it is covered by an incomplete membrane known as the hymen.

8. The hymen is a membrane, present from birth, which partially closes the vaginal orifice. The central portion is defective so that a hole is present which allows the menstrual discharge to drain away.

The hymen is usually ruptured at the time of first intercourse but it varies considerably in elasticity. Further lacerations occur during childbirth. It then becomes represented by small fleshy tags which surround the vaginal orifice and are called carunculae myrtiformes.

A small depression between the hymen and the fourchette is known as the fossa navicularis.

9. The vestibular bulbs (Fig. 1/2) are two small collections of vascular erectile tissue which lie on either side of the vaginal opening, deep to the labia majora and minora, and anterior to Bartholin's glands. They become thinner as they pass forwards, where they unite above the urethral orifice to become continuous with the glans of the clitoris.

10. Bartholin's glands (Fig. 1/2) are two compound racemose glands, about the size and shape of small beans, which lie on either side of the posterior part of the vaginal opening, behind the vestibular bulbs and deep to the labia. When enlarged they can be palpated in the posterior third of the labia majora.

The ducts from the glands are lined by transitional epithelium and pass inwards and open on the surface just external to the hymen and medial to the labia minora.

Their function is to excrete mucus which keeps the external genital organs moist and lubricated.

Both the vestibular bulbs and Bartholin's glands rest upon a deeper structure known as the triangular ligament or the perineal membrane.


The vulva is supplied with blood from two main arteries:

1. The femoral artery, in the upper part of the thigh. This sends branches known as the superficial and deep external pudendal arteries into the vulva.

2. The internal pudendal artery, running along the pubic arch. This terminates in branches which supply the vulva, known as the posterior labial and the deep and dorsal arteries of the clitoris.

The veins drain to corresponding veins.

Lymphatic vessels pass to the horizontal groups of inguinal glands, some passing directly to the external iliac groups.

The skin of the vulva is supplied by the ilio-inguinal nerve, the genital branch of the genito-femoral nerve and the perineal branch of the posterior cutaneous nerve of the thigh. It also receives branches from the posterior labial nerves and the dorsal nerve of the clitoris, which are derived from the pudendal nerve.

## THE VAGINA

The vagina is a tube which leads from the vulva to the uterus, passing upwards and backwards into the pelvis, approximately parallel to the plane of the pelvic brim. It is partially closed at its lower end (in virgins) by the hymen. At its upper end it is attached to the cervix of the uterus, which projects almost at a right angle into the upper part of its anterior wall, thus making the posterior wall of the vagina longer (10.1cm) than the anterior wall (7.6cm). The recesses of the vagina which surround the projecting cervix are named the fornices of the vagina. They are four in number, and are known, according to their positions, as the anterior, posterior and lateral fornices. As the vagina is attached to the cervix at a higher level behind than in front, it makes the posterior fornix larger and more voluminous than either the anterior fornix or the two lateral fornices.

Although the vagina is here described as a tube its lumen is not normally patent, but instead the anterior and posterior walls lie in close contact. They easily become separated to allow the passage of blood during menstruation and the fetus during parturition.

### Structure
On inspection the vaginal walls are seen to be pink in colour. Their texture is not smooth as they are composed of numerous transverse small folds or ridges, which are known as rugae. Their function is to enable the vagina to enlarge. This occurs during parturition when they become stretched out and obliterated, thereby allowing the vagina to accommodate the fetus during its passage to the vulva.

The walls are composed of the following structures:

a) A layer of stratified squamous epithelium, which lines the cavity of the vagina.

b) A vascular layer of elastic connective tissue.

c) A layer of involuntary muscle fibres arranged in a criss-cross manner.

d) An encircling layer of connective tissue, containing blood vessels, lymphatics and nerves, which is part of the visceral pelvic fascia.

### Contents
There are no glands situated in the walls of the vagina, which cannot therefore be said to have a lining of mucous membrane. The vagina,

however, contains a small amount of fluid which is derived from two sources: it comes partly from the glands of the cervix which excrete an alkaline mucus, and partly from the vaginal blood vessels which allow serous fluid to transude through the vaginal walls into its lumen. Despite the alkalinity of the cervical mucus the vaginal fluid is acid in reaction having a pH of about 4.5 during reproductive life—this is due to the presence of lactic acid in a concentration of 0.3 per cent. It is produced by bacterial action on glycogen which is released from the cells of the squamous epithelium lining the vagina. These organisms are known as Döderlein's bacilli, and are normal inhabitants of the healthy vagina. If they are absent or reduced in number, as occurs in youth and old age, the vagina is less acid, or even alkaline, and infections such as vulvo-vaginitis in young girls and senile vaginitis in elderly women are prone to occur.

This vaginal acidity has a useful function, for any pathogenic organisms which may invade the vagina are largely destroyed, so maintaining the upper part of the genital tract in a healthy state free from harmful bacteria.

### Relations
The vagina has important anatomical relations (Fig. 1/3):

*Anterior.* The bladder and the urethra.

*Posterior.* The perineal body forms the immediate relation of the lowest third of the posterior wall, and separates it from the anal canal.

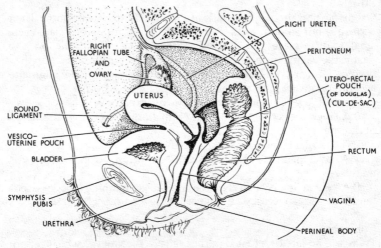

**Fig. 1/3:**   Sagittal section of the female pelvis

The posterior relation of the middle third is the rectum itself, while behind the upper third of the posterior wall lies the peritoneum forming the pouch of Douglas.

*Lateral*. The upper two-thirds of the vagina are related laterally to the pelvic fascia at the base of the broad ligaments, embedded in which run blood vessels, lymphatics and nerves. The two ureters pass close to the lateral fornices on their way to the bladder.

The lateral relations of the lowest third are mainly muscular, consisting of the two levator ani muscles which pass on either side of the vagina, and the bulbo-cavernosus muscles which lie below them, encircling the introitus vaginae. The vestibular bulbs and Bartholin's glands are also lateral relations of the vaginal opening.

*Superior*. The upper relation of the vagina is the uterus, the cervix being inserted into the upper part of its anterior wall.

*Inferior*. Below the vagina lie the hymen or the carunculae myrtiformes and the structures of the vulva.

The blood supply to the vagina comes from the vaginal, the uterine (descending branch), the middle haemorrhoidal, the inferior vesical and pudendal arteries—all branches of the internal iliac artery. The veins drain in a corresponding manner.

The lymphatics of the lowest third drain to the horizontal inguinal groups along with those of the vulva; from the upper two-thirds they pass to the internal iliac and sacral glands.

The nerve supply is from the sympathetic and pelvic splanchnics.


## THE UTERUS

The uterus is a hollow, flattened, muscular, pear-shaped organ which lies in the true pelvis above the vagina, receiving the insertions of the two Fallopian tubes into its upper and outer angles (Fig. 1/4). It measures 7.6cm in length, 5.1cm in width at its widest part and 2.5cm in depth, while its walls are 1.3cm in thickness. The uterine cavity is therefore 6.4cm long. The uterus weighs about 56g. It consists of the following parts:

a) The body or corpus, which comprises the upper two-thirds of the uterus. The cavity of the body is triangular in shape with its base directed upwards. Owing to the flattening of the uterus, its anterior and posterior walls are normally in contact.

b) The neck or cervix, which forms the lowest third of the uterus and is therefore 2.5cm in length. The cavity here is narrow and slightly fusiform in shape, being known as the cervical canal. Its widest part lies in the centre of the cervix, and it is more constricted above where it

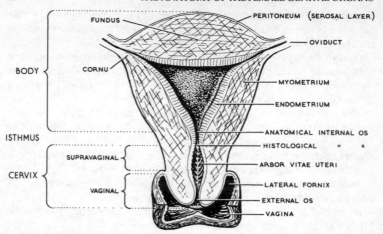

**Fig. 1/4:**   Coronal section of uterus

is continuous with the cavity of the body through the internal os, and below where it communicates with the vagina through the external os.

c) The isthmus, which is a narrow zone of the corpus uteri, about 7mm in length, situated in its lowest part immediately above the internal os, lying between the body and the cervix. It has a special function during pregnancy (see Chapter 8).

d) The fundus, which is the portion of the body of the uterus lying between the insertions of the two Fallopian tubes.

e) The cornua, which is the name applied to the lateral angles of the uterine body where the Fallopian tubes are attached.

**Structure**

The uterus is a muscular organ, and its walls are chiefly composed of plain muscle cells. This part of the uterus is known as the myometrium. The uterine cavity is lined by mucous membrane which is called the endometrium.

*The Endometrium*

This is the mucous membrane which lines the interior of the uterus. The mucosa of the uterine body (Fig. 1/4) differs markedly from that of the cervical canal, their chief features being as follows:

*The corporeal endometrium* consists of vascular connective tissue, known as the stroma, in which are contained numerous mucus secreting tubular glands which open into the uterine cavity. The stroma is covered by a layer of cubical cells which form the glands by dipping down in finger-like processes into the stroma. These cells are ciliated on the surface. The endometrium varies in thickness and vascularity from day to day according to the phases of the menstrual cycle, and it is largely shed during the actual process of menstruation (see Chapter 4). The endometrium of the isthmus is thinner than that of the rest of the corpus, and as it has fewer glands and blood vessels, is of generally poorer quality.

*The cervical endometrium* is much thinner than that of the body. It is made up of a connective tissue stroma lined by tall ciliated columnar cells with basal nuclei which rests on the muscle and collagen of the cervix. There is no submucosa present. In places the epithelium forms deep branching glands, known as compound racemose glands, which penetrate deeply into the underlying tissue. Their function is to secrete mucus the quality and quantity of which is under hormone control.

The cervical endometrium is raised into folds or ridges: one of these runs down the anterior wall of the cervical canal and one down the posterior, while parallel branches radiate from both in upward and lateral directions. This formation is known as the arbor vitae.

## The Myometrium
This constitutes the main mass of the uterus, and in the body is made up of plain muscle cells which run in bundles separated by connective tissue. The muscle bundles pass in all directions in an interlacing manner (when the patient is not pregnant), and surround the blood vessels and lymphatics passing to and from the endometrium. The outermost muscle fibres become continuous with those of the uterine ligaments and the longitudinal fibres of the Fallopian tubes and vagina.

In the cervix, however, the muscle bundles are less numerous and compact, and they lie embedded in a groundwork of collagen fibres. Some muscle fibres form a continuous band running from the body of the uterus to the vagina, which constitutes the 'extrinsic' muscle of the cervix; other more immature fibres radiate towards the mucosa and the lips of the cervix, and comprise the 'intrinsic' muscle.

## The Perimetrium
This is the outer covering of the uterus which consists of peritoneum. A full description of the distribution of the pelvic peritoneum is given later.

### Attachments
1. The vagina is related to the uterus below, where the cervix projects into its upper part and so creates the vaginal fornices. The

vaginal wall is attached half-way along the length of the cervix, so that it becomes divided into two approximately equal halves, the supra-vaginal cervix situated above the vagina, and the vaginal cervix lying within its lumen. The vaginal portion of the cervix is covered by squamous epithelium similar to that which lines the vagina itself; this becomes continuous with the columnar epithelium of the cervical canal at the external os.

2. At the upper part of the uterus the Fallopian tubes are attached to the uterus in the regions of the cornua.

3. The upper two-thirds of the vagina and the cervix are surrounded by visceral pelvic fascia, which may be thought of as packing material, filling the spaces between the various pelvic organs. In places this fascia becomes condensed into strong bands which run from the uterus and the vagina to the pelvic walls. These bands contain smooth muscle fibres which have contractile and supporting functions; they are known as uterine ligaments and help to maintain this organ in its normal position (Fig. 1/5).

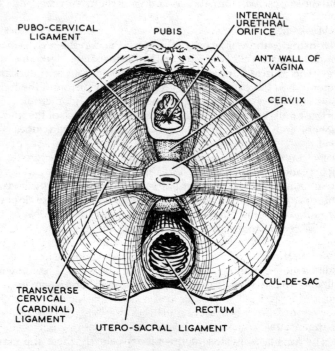

**Fig. 1/5:**   The supporting ligaments from above

## The Uterine Ligaments

1. The two cardinal ligaments, also known as the transverse cervical ligaments and Mackenrodt's ligaments, run in a radiating fan-like manner from the lateral aspect of the cervix below the level of the internal os and the lateral fornices of the vagina to the side walls of the pelvis, where they are attached to the fascia overlying the obturator internus muscles. The ureters on their way to the bladder pass through these ligaments, lying in what are known as the ureteric canals.

2. The two utero-sacral ligaments pass from the cervix in an upward and backward direction, and encircle the rectum to become attached to the periosteum of the sacrum.

3. The two pubo-cervical ligaments are a pair of weak ligaments which run forwards from the cervix, underneath the bladder, to become attached to the pubic bones. Some authorities deny that they exist.

4. The two round ligaments begin at the cornua of the uterus, pass downwards, forwards and outwards within the broad ligaments, and then cross the lateral parts of the pelvic floor to reach the internal inguinal rings, situated above the inguinal ligaments in the anterior abdominal wall. They then turn medially around the deep epigastric vessels and enter the inguinal canals in the groins. They traverse the canals, emerge through the external rings in the oblique muscles, and end in the fatty tissues of the labia majora.

These ligaments are of embryological interest, for they mark the route along which the testes descend in the male, in whom the scrotum corresponds to the fused labia majora.

5. The two ovarian ligaments also begin at the cornua of the uterus and pass downwards, backwards and outwards inside the broad ligaments for about 2.5cm to become connected to the ovaries. They help to suspend the ovaries in their normal position and keep them steady while ovulation is occurring.

The ovarian and round ligaments form one continuous ligament during early fetal life, and are derived from a common origin, known as the gubernaculum ovarii.

6. The two broad ligaments. Although these are mentioned here for the sake of completeness, it must be clearly understood that they are not condensations of pelvic fascia, but are folds of peritoneum passing laterally from the uterus to the side walls of the pelvis. They are not true ligaments in any way, and are more fully described later.

The uterus and pelvic cellular tissue lie in the pelvis above the levator ani muscles which form a platform to support them in their normal positions. When these muscles relax, as during defaecation, the ligaments act as direct supports of the uterus, the most important in this way being the cardinal ligaments.

## Position

The uterus is situated in the true pelvis between the bladder in front and below (Fig. 1/6) and the pouch of Douglas and rectum behind. The cervix lies approximately on an imaginary line joining the ischial spines. In 80 per cent of individuals the uterus inclines forwards over the upper surface of the bladder, and is said to lie in a position of anteversion.

The maintenance of this position is helped by the supporting action of the utero-sacral ligaments behind and the round ligaments in front. In 20 per cent of individuals the reverse position is present and the uterus then inclines backwards, this being known as retroversion.

In addition to this inclination, the body of the uterus may bend forwards or backwards on the cervix at the level of the internal os. This is known as anteflexion or retroflexion of the uterus respectively—the former is the commoner.

## Relations

*Anterior.* The bladder is placed anterior to the cervix with the pubo-cervical ligaments below it. The utero-vesical pouch of peritoneum and coils of intestine lie in front of the body, above the bladder.

*Posterior* (Fig. 1/7). The posterior surface of the uterus is in relation to the peritoneal cavity, the portion lying below the utero-sacral folds of peritoneum being known as the pouch of Douglas. The utero-sacral ligaments are also posterior relations.

*Lateral.* Lateral to the body of the uterus are the broad ligaments, the Fallopian tubes, ovaries and round ligaments.

Lateral to the cervix, running in the pelvic fascia, lie the ureters which are passing forwards to the bladder; alongside the cervix they are crossed above by the uterine vessels which are passing from the side walls of the pelvis to supply the uterus.

*Superior.* The intestines.

*Inferior.* The vagina. The fornices can be said to form the immediate relations of the vaginal cervix.

The blood supply of the body of the uterus comes from the uterine and ovarian arteries and returns via corresponding veins. The cervix is supplied by descending branches from the uterine arteries and is drained by the uterine veins.

The lymph drainage of the body is into the internal iliac glands, with small vessels passing along the round ligaments to the horizontal inguinal glands. Lymph from the cervix drains first into the para-metrial glands, lying alongside the cervix in the visceral pelvic fascia, and then to the internal iliac and sacral glands. A few lymphatic vessels

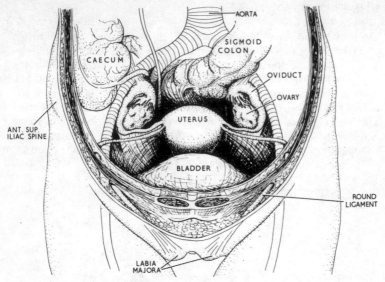

**Fig. 1/6:** Anterior view of uterus and bladder

pass first to the obturator glands lying in the obturator fossa in the upper part of the foramen ovale and then to the internal iliac glands.

The nerve supply is from the sympathetic and parasympathetic systems.

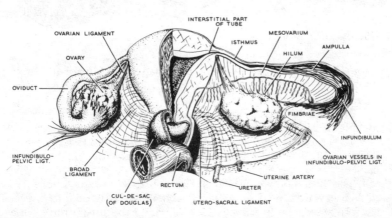

**Fig. 1/7:** Posterior view of uterus

## THE FALLOPIAN TUBES

These are two small tubes, each about 10cm long and 6mm in diameter, which are attached to the cornua of the uterus. They pass laterally from the uterus across the pelvis almost to reach its side walls, where they turn backwards and downwards towards the ovaries. The tubes possess a lumen which communicates with the cavity of the uterus medially and which opens into the peritoneal cavity laterally. The female genital tract is thus an open pathway which leads from the exterior to the peritoneal cavity via the vulva, vagina, uterus and Fallopian tubes.

The tubes consist of four parts (Fig. 1/8):

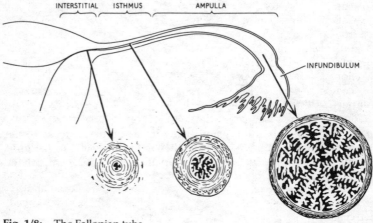

**Fig. 1/8:**    The Fallopian tube

1. The interstitial part, which is the narrowest part of the tube, having a lumen of one millimetre, lying within the thickness of the uterine wall.

2. The isthmus, which also is a narrow portion of the tube extending for about 2.5cm laterally from the uterine wall.

3. The ampulla, which is much wider than the isthmus and extends for about 5.0cm laterally from the isthmus towards the side wall of the pelvis.

4. The infundibulum, which is the lateral 2.5cm of the tube which turns backwards and downwards. It is composed of numerous finger-like processes, the fimbriae, which surround the tubal orifice. One fimbria is attached to the ovary.

## Attachments

The tubes are attached medially to the uterus, and as they pass transversely across the pelvis they carry with them the peritoneum. This is draped across them forming a fold which passes down to the pelvic floor below, so constituting the broad ligaments.

Where the lateral extremities of the tubes bend backwards, the peritoneum is continued as folds to the side walls of the pelvis, producing what are known as the infundibulo-pelvic ligaments. It can thus be appreciated that these are peritoneal structures and not true ligaments, although they do accord some means of support both to the Fallopian tubes and ovaries. They also transmit the ovarian vessels, lymphatics and nerves.

## Structure

The Fallopian tube is a true tube although this would hardly be suspected from looking at its cross-section under the microscope, because its mucous membrane is thrown into such rich and profuse folds that its lumen is not obvious. These folds, which are known as plicae, are most developed in the ampullary portions of the tubes, where they act as a device which serves to slow down the passage of the ovum during its journey to the uterus.

The parts of the tube outside the uterus are made up of the following layers:

1. A layer of cubical epithelium, many cells of which are ciliated, which covers the plicae throughout all their intricacies. Some of the non-ciliated cells are known as goblet cells and contain large globules of secretion; these are discharged into the lumen of the tube shortly before menstruation, after which the cells collapse and are then called peg cells.

2. A vascular layer of connective tissue, which lies below the surface epithelium.

3. An inner layer of circular smooth muscle which surrounds the mucous membrane.

4. An outer layer of longitudinal smooth muscle.

5. An outer covering of peritoneum, which is absent along the inferior surface of the tube between the layers of the broad ligament.

## Relations

*Medial.* The uterus.

*Lateral.* The infundibulo-pelvic ligaments and the side walls of the pelvis.

*Anterior, superior and posterior.* The peritoneal cavity and the intestines.

*Inferior.* The broad ligaments and ovaries.

The tubes are supplied with blood from the uterine and ovarian arteries, and drain via corresponding veins.

The lymphatics pass with those of the ovary to the lumbar glands.

The nerve supply is mainly from the ovarian plexus.

## THE OVARIES

The ovary is an organ whose structure and function vary at different ages of the individual. These changes are described in Chapter 4, and the anatomical description now given is that of the ovary during the child-bearing period of life.

The ovaries are two small almond-shaped bodies, dull white in colour and corrugated on the surface, measuring 3cm in length, 2cm in breadth and 1cm in thickness and weighing about 6g. They are attached to the posterior layer of the broad ligaments, and lie inside the peritoneal cavity. The lateral portion of the Fallopian tube arches over the ovary and ends in close proximity to it, being connected to it by the fimbriae. When the uterus is retroverted the ovaries may lie in the pouch of Douglas.

### Attachments

The place of attachment of the ovary to the posterior layer of the broad ligament is known as the mesovarium, and the part of the broad ligament extending above this point to the Fallopian tube is called the mesosalpinx.

This attachment however is too weak to support the ovary, which is suspended from the uterine cornu by the ovarian ligament. This is a strong structure, containing smooth muscle, which runs inside the broad ligament to be attached to the ovary through the medial margin of the mesovarium.

Similarly the lateral pole of the ovary is supported by the infundi-bulo-pelvic ligament, which has already been described as a fold of peritoneum running to the side wall of the pelvis and transmitting the ovarian vessels, lymphatics and nerves.

### Structure

The ovary consists of a medulla and cortex surrounded by a layer of germinal epithelium.

1. The medulla is the part of the ovary which is directly attached to the broad ligament at the mesovarium. It consists of fibrous tissue and transmits the ovarian vessels, lymphatics and nerves which enter and

leave the ovary from the broad ligament, which they have reached through the infundibulo-pelvic ligament.

2. The cortex is the functional part of the ovary and consists of a dense stroma in which are situated ovarian follicles and corpora lutea in various stages of development and retrogression (see Chapter 4). The outer part of the cortex is formed by a dense fibrous coat, which is known as the tunica albuginea.

3. The germinal epithelium consists of a layer of low cubical cells which covers the tunica albuginea of the cortex, and is continuous with the peritoneum of the broad ligament at the mesovarium. It may be said to be a modified form of the peritoneum which covers the ovary.

### Relations

*Medial.* The body of the uterus and the ovarian ligament running to the cornu.

*Lateral.* The infundibulo-pelvic ligament and the side wall of the pelvis, covered by parietal peritoneum.

*Anterior.* The broad ligament and the mesovarium.

*Posterior.* The peritoneal cavity and the intestines.

The blood supply is from the ovarian arteries. The ovarian veins join the inferior vena cava on the right and the left renal vein on the left.

The lymph drainage is into the lumbar glands.

The nerve supply is from the ovarian plexus.


## THE PELVIC PERITONEUM

The anatomy of the female internal genital organs cannot be properly understood unless their relation to the distribution of the pelvic peritoneum is clearly borne in mind (Fig. 1/9). This is somewhat complex in the female and is best learnt by comparison with its distribution in the more simple male pelvis.

In males, the peritoneum lines the anterior abdominal wall, extends down on to the upper surface of the bladder and then passes on to the rectum and the posterior abdominal wall. In the female pelvis the uterus, tubes and ovaries are placed transversely across the pelvis between the bladder and rectum; consequently the peritoneum first passes on to the upper surface of the bladder, then passes up the anterior surface of the uterus, over the fundus and down the posterior surface as far as the junction of the upper and middle thirds of the posterior wall of the vagina. It then passes on to the rectum and posterior abdominal wall as in the male. The uterus, however, only occupies the median plane of the pelvis and the Fallopian tubes spread

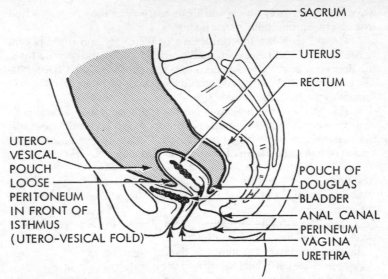

**Fig. 1/9:**  Sagittal section of the female pelvis showing the pelvic peritoneum

out on either side of it as far as the lateral pelvic walls. Consequently, lateral to the uterus, the peritoneum rises up to the Fallopian tubes, arches over their upper border and then descends behind them, so forming the broad ligaments. The uterus and broad ligaments thus form a partition across the pelvis which divides it into anterior and posterior compartments. Certain details of this arrangement are to be specially noted:

1. In the anterior compartment the pouch between the upper surface of the bladder and the uterus is known as the utero-vesical pouch. It is placed at the level of the internal os of the uterus and does not come into direct relation with the vagina.

2. In the posterior compartment the pouch between the uterus and rectum is the pouch of Douglas. It is in direct relation with the upper third of the vagina. The folds of peritoneum which lie above the utero-sacral ligaments and form the lateral margins of the pouch are known as the utero-sacral folds.

3. The uterus is covered everywhere with peritoneum except:
    (a)  A narrow strip along each lateral border, corresponding to the space between the layers of the broad ligament.
    (b)  The front of the supra-vaginal cervix, below the level of the utero-vesical pouch.
    (c)  The vaginal portion of the cervix.

4. It is to be noted that the peritoneum is attached very loosely to the front of the isthmus of the uterus above the level of the internal os, but quite firmly elsewhere. This is to allow the peritoneum to accommodate itself to the distended bladder when it becomes filled with urine.

5. The peritoneum covers the upper two-thirds of the rectum, lining its anterior aspect in the middle third, and its anterior and lateral aspects in the upper third. The lowest third lies posterior to the middle third of the vagina and is not related to the peritoneum.

## The Contents of the Broad Ligament

The space between the two peritoneal layers forming the broad ligament is filled with visceral pelvic fascia and fat, containing the uterine and ovarian vessels and their branches, lymphatics and nerves. In addition other important structures are present:

1. The Fallopian tube in its upper border.
2. The ovarian ligament.
3. The round ligament.
4. The ureter. This passes forwards through the base of the broad ligament lateral to the cervix, close to the lateral fornix of the vagina. In this position it passes through Mackenrodt's ligament in a special tunnel, known as the ureteric canal.
5. The epoöphoron, paroöphoron and Gärtner's duct are embryonic structures, corresponding to the ducts of the male reproductive system, which persist in a rudimentary fashion in the female. They are present in the mesosalpinx, and Gärtner's duct, when well formed, runs down the lateral border of the uterus into the lateral wall of the vagina.

*Chapter Two*

# The Anatomy and Physiology of the Renal Tract: Other Pelvic Organs

## ANATOMY OF THE KIDNEY

The kidneys are two organs of characteristic shape which lie outside the peritoneum on the posterior abdominal wall, one on each side of the vertebral column. They measure 10cm in length, 6.4cm in width, and 3.1cm in thickness and each weighs about 114g. They extend from the upper border of the twelfth thoracic vertebra to the third lumbar vertebra with the upper pole slightly closer to the middle line than the lower pole. The centre of the inner border is connected by a vascular pedicle with the descending aorta and the inferior vena cava—this lies at the level of the intervertebral disc between the first and second

A

B

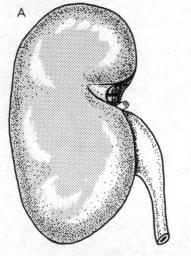
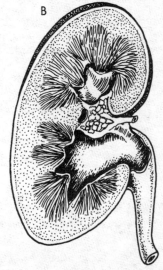

**Fig. 2/1:**   A.  Anterior aspect of right kidney
B.  Section of right kidney

lumbar vertebrae. The right kidney is placed at a slightly lower level than the left, owing to the presence of the liver in the right hypochondrium.

The kidney is smooth in outline, reddish-brown in colour, with convex surfaces and broadly rounded margins (Fig. 2/1A&B). The upper and lower poles are almost semicircular, while the lateral border is gently curved. The medial border is indented in its middle third, a region known as the hilum, where the renal artery enters and the renal vein and ureter leave the kidney. These structures, together with lymphatic vessels and nerves, comprise the renal pedicles. The hilum consists of a cleft lying between thick rounded lips into which these structures pass, the vein, artery and ureter lying in that order from before backwards.

## Relations

*Anterior*. The kidneys lie in relation to the contents of the abdomen, which are different on the two sides (Fig. 2/2):

(a) *The left kidney.* The inner aspect of the upper pole is surmounted

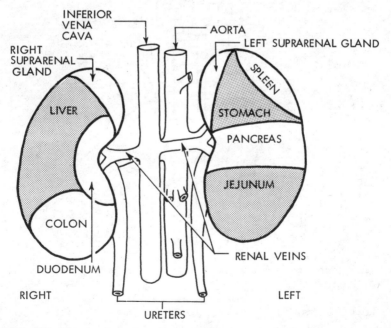

**Fig. 2/2:**  The anterior relations of the kidneys

by the left suprarenal gland, while the outer aspect is related to the spleen. Extending as a horizontal band across the central region lies the pancreas, the triangular area thus demarcated between these organs forming part of the bed of the stomach. The lower pole, below the pancreatic area, lies in relation to the jejunum.

(b) *The right kidney.* In a similar manner the inner aspect of the upper pole is related to the right suprarenal gland, while the area surrounding the hilum lies behind the duodenum. The liver lies in front of the upper half of the remainder of the anterior surface, while the hepatic flexure of the colon is in contact with the lower half.

*Posterior.* The kidneys lie in relation to the structures of the posterior abdominal wall, which, apart from the slight lowering of the right kidney, are identical on the two sides (Fig. 2/3).

The upper half of each kidney rests against the diaphragm, the twelfth rib passing obliquely outwards and downwards across its

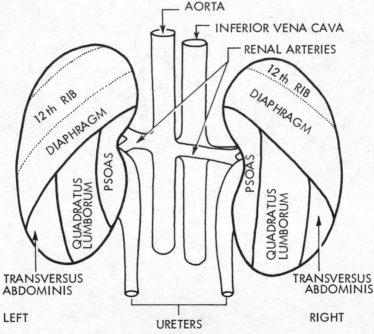

**Fig. 2/3:** The posterior relations of the kidneys

surface, but separated from it by the diaphragmatic muscle fibres. Between the diaphragm and the rib the pleural cavity is a posterior relation, especially on the left side where the kidney is higher.

The lower half of the kidney lies against three muscles of the posterior abdominal wall, which, passing outwards from the spine, are the psoas major, the quadratus lumborum, and the transversus abdominis.

## Supports

The kidney is closely covered by a thick fibrous capsule, and lies embedded in loose cellular tissue containing copious deposits of fat, known as the perinephric fat. It is supported in this position by:

1. The general intra-abdominal pressure and close contact with adjoining organs.

2. The attachment of the vessels to the aorta and the inferior vena cava.

3. An investment of deep fascia, connected below to the parietal pelvic fascia, which surrounds the kidney. This is attached by fibrous strands to the kidney capsule, and is known in this situation as the renal fascia.

## The Kidney on Section

If the kidney is divided from its lateral border towards the hilum, and its two halves are opened out, its naked eye structure can be seen. It will be noted that the ureter opens into a cavity known as the pelvis of the kidney, and that the surrounding kidney is divided into two zones. The inner of these is pale in colour and is known as the medulla, while the outer zone is reddish-brown and of uniform consistency and is called the cortex. The following features are to be noted:

*The pelvis of the kidney* has an intimate relation with the medulla. It divides into large branches known as the major calyces, and these in their turn subdivide into smaller branches called the minor calyces into which portions of the medulla protrude.

*The medulla* consists of about twelve small conical masses which project into the minor calyces of the renal pelvis, with their base extending to about half-way towards the surface. They contain faint parallel streaks which run towards the tip of the projection. These constitute the pyramids of the kidney, while the streaks terminating in their apices are known as the medullary rays. These are the collecting tubules which carry urine from the cortex of the kidney to the calyces. From here the urine passes into the pelvis of the kidney and then makes its journey down the ureter into the bladder.

*The cortex* arches over the bases of the pyramids, lying between them and the surface, and in places extends between them to reach to the pelvis.

*The capsule* is a thick fibrous coat which surrounds the cortex, from which it can be stripped. In the body it is attached to the surrounding renal fascia and perinephric fat. Running underneath it external to the cortex lies a series of veins known as the stellate veins.

*The renal blood vessels.* After the renal artery enters the kidney it divides into branches which form arches lying between the cortex and the medulla. These give off small arterioles which enter and supply the cortex. Venous blood is collected into similar arches lying in the boundary between the cortex and medulla, which also receive blood from the stellate veins. They finally unite to form the renal vein.

### The Structure of the Kidney

The chief kidney function is to regulate the composition and volume of the blood plasma, which it does by secreting urine, and its structure is designed primarily for this purpose. The urine is produced by about a million small units in each kidney known as nephrons, which are packed closely together in a connecting stroma thereby forming a solid mass which is the kidney substance. It is convenient to study the

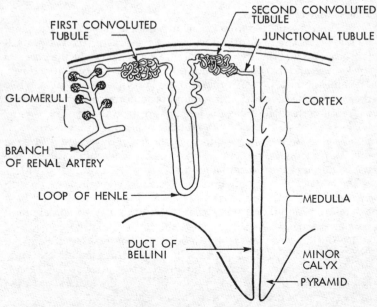

**Fig. 2/4:**   Structure of a nephron

minute anatomy of one of these structures, the nephron (Fig. 2/4), and its intimate association with the renal blood vessels.

It has already been stated that the renal artery sends branches into the cortex, and as these extend towards the capsule they give off small arterioles which break up into globular clumps of capillaries known as glomeruli. Each of these is invested around its periphery by a thin membrane formed of flat epithelial cells which is reflected back on itself to produce a cup-like structure. The glomerulus thus invaginates the membrane which is called Bowman's capsule. From this capsule a small tubule, known as a uriniferous tubule, arises. The glomerulus, surrounded by Bowman's capsule, forms what is known as a Malpighian body (Fig. 2/5). The vessel carrying blood into the

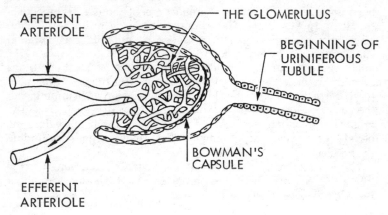

**Fig. 2/5:** Structure of a Malpighian body

glomerulus is called the afferent arteriole, and the vessel draining blood away from it is the efferent arteriole. Here are therefore two arterioles, one which delivers blood into the glomerular capillaries, and one which drains it away.

After leaving the Malpighian body the uriniferous tubule does not branch, but instead takes a tortuous course, twisting and turning in all directions within the cortex. This part of its course is known as the first or proximal convoluted tubule of the nephron. The cubical cells by which it is lined contain particles arranged in parallel rows along the surface. The border of the cells lining the lumen of the tubule thus has a striated appearance which is known as the brush border.

After a series of these convolutions the tubule takes a spiral course, where it is known as the spiral tubule, and then straightens out and dips down into the medulla. It travels a short distance and then makes a U-turn and returns to the cortex. This formation is known as the loop of Henle, and the two limbs of the loop comprise its descending and ascending limbs. The cells lining these limbs differ. Thus the descending limb and the U-bend are lined by flattened cells but have a narrow lumen, while the ascending limb contains cubical cells and is much wider.

After returning to the cortex, the tubule takes a crooked course, where it is called the zig-zag tubule, after which a second series of convolutions follows forming the second or distal convoluted tubule. On leaving the convolutions the tubule is called a junctional tubule, which then joins a collecting tubule. This runs from the cortex to the apex of the pyramid, forming the medullary rays which have already been noted, and receiving the terminations of about 4 200 junctional tubules during its course. These are also known as the ducts of Bellini. They open into a minor calyx at the apex of a pyramid, each pyramid containing about twenty ducts.

The efferent arteriole, after leaving the glomerulus, breaks up into a second network of capillaries which surrounds the tubules throughout their course. These ultimately join to form venules, which uniting with the stellate veins from the capsule, finally form the renal veins. The original arteriole thus gives rise to two sets of capillaries before the blood joins the vein, one forming the glomerulus and one surrounding the tubules.

The length of each tubule is about 3cm, so that the total length of the tubules of the two million nephrons in the two kidneys is about thirty-eight miles (60 kilometres).

## Lymphatic Supply
A plexus of lymph vessels lies beneath the kidney capsule which is connected to a second plexus surrounding the uriniferous tubules. Lymphatic trunks emerge from these plexuses and follow the renal vein to end in the aortic or lumbar lymphatic glands.

## Nerve Supply
The kidney is supplied by sympathetic and para-sympathetic nerves coming from the renal plexus, which is derived from the coeliac and aortic plexuses and the splanchnic nerves lying on the posterior abdominal wall. Branches accompany the renal artery into the substance of the kidney and are distributed to the blood vessels throughout their ramifications.

The renal plexus sends branches which communicate with the ovarian plexus.

## PHYSIOLOGY OF THE KIDNEY

### The Formation of Urine

The chief function of the kidney is to regulate the composition and volume of the blood plasma by secreting urine, which it does by virtue of the structure described previously. Thus blood at high pressure is delivered into the glomerulus from the aorta, via the renal artery and the afferent arteriole. Here the fluid part of the blood, consisting of water and dissolved salts and ions, passes through Bowman's capsule into the upper part of the uriniferous tubule. It will be noted that the solid particles in the blood (red and white corpuscles and platelets), together with protein molecules, do not pass through this barrier but leave the glomerulus by the efferent arteriole. Considering the high pressure of blood coming directly from the aorta (about 75mm Hg in the glomerulus), and the great number of nephrons, it would be expected that a large volume of fluid would enter the uriniferous tubules in the course of twenty-four hours—this is certainly true, as some 170 litres are filtered off from the blood in this way per day.

The fluid (known as the glomerular filtrate) then passes along the whole length of the tubule, and during this journey the greater part of the water, and all the dissolved substances which are of value to the body, are re-absorbed by the cells lining the tubules and are passed back into the circulation. Only waste products of no value to the individual pass on to the collecting tubules and then into the pelvis of the kidney. In this way 168.5 litres of fluid are re-absorbed, leaving only 1.5 litres to pass down the ureter into the bladder and constitute the urine.

Thus sugar and bicarbonates, and sodium, chloride and calcium ions, are filtered off by the glomeruli but are largely re-absorbed by the tubules; urea, urates, uric acid, sulphates and phosphates which are also filtered off are only re-absorbed to a slight extent and so appear in the urine. The tubular cells thus have the power of re-absorbing substances selectively, according to the body's requirements. Some compounds such as creatinine and ingested toxic substances are excreted by the tubular cells directly into the urine. The function of the tubules therefore is mainly re-absorptive but is partly excretory. The re-absorption takes place chiefly in the ascending limb of the loop of Henle. The re-absorption of water is largely under the control of anti-diuretic hormone (ADH), derived from the posterior lobe of the pituitary gland, while the re-absorption of sodium ions (which occurs in the second convoluted tubule) is controlled by a hormone known as aldosterone, derived from the suprarenal cortex.

**Kidney Functions in Detail**

1. By this process of urinary formation the kidneys regulate the volume of plasma in the blood and the amount of fluid in the extra-cellular spaces of the tissues. It is well recognised that the more fluid drunk and absorbed, the larger is the volume of urine excreted, while if much fluid is lost by perspiration or diarrhoea, the urinary output is reduced.

2. The reaction of the blood is kept constant by a similar mechanism. If the hydrogen ion concentration of the blood is increased producing a tendency towards acidity, the ions are excreted in acid urine, in the form of acid phosphate, and the pH of the blood remains constant. Conversely if the hydrogen ion concentration is reduced, alkaline urine, containing alkaline phosphate and possibly bicarbonate, is produced.

3. Waste products are excreted in the urine, particularly urea, urates, uric acid, ammonia, creatinine and sulphates, which are all the end-products of protein metabolism.

4. Toxic substances introduced into the body are eliminated.

5. By means of these excretory functions the kidneys regulate the osmotic pressure of the blood and tissue fluids.

6. The cortex secretes a hormone known as renin. This is produced when the blood supply to the kidney is reduced; it combines with a protein called hypertensinogen present in the blood to form a pressor agent, hypertensin or angiotonin, which brings about a rise in blood pressure.

7. The kidneys secrete another hormone into the blood stream that stimulates the formation of red blood cells in the marrow. This is known as renal erythropoietin. A reduced secretion, occurring in cases of chronic nephritis, accounts for the anaemia that accompanies this disease.

The kidneys thus have mainly a regulatory and excretory function; they are essential to life and the individual cannot live for long if their function becomes seriously deranged.

## THE URETERS

The ureters are two narrow tubes, about 25.4cm in length and 3mm in diameter, which convey the urine from the pelves of the kidneys to the bladder. They are essentially muscular in nature, and waves of peristalsis pass along them propelling the urine into the bladder, in much the same way that the gut contents are driven forwards by intestinal peristalsis.

**Structure**

The wall of the ureter as it passes through the pelvis is composed of the following layers:

1. A coat of transitional epithelium which lines the lumen of the tube and forms longitudinal folds.

2. A fibrous tissue layer containing many elastic fibres, on which the epithelium rests.

3. An inner weak layer of longitudinal smooth muscle fibres.

4. A middle circular layer of smooth muscle.

5. A well-defined outer layer of longitudinal muscle.

6. A coat of fibrous connective tissue.

**Course**

Throughout their whole course the ureters are placed outside the peritoneum (Fig. 2/6).

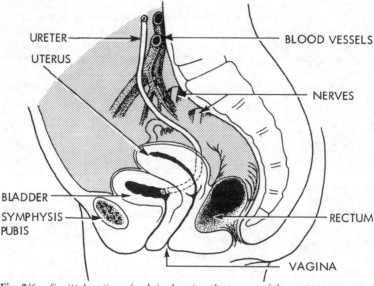

**Fig. 2/6:**   Sagittal section of pelvis showing the course of the ureter

They begin at the kidneys and pass down in the posterior abdominal wall towards the pelvis. They cross the pelvic brim anterior to the sacro-iliac joint and enter the true pelvis by passing over the common iliac arteries at the point where these divide into the external and internal iliac arteries. The ureters then pass down the side walls of the pelvis lying in front of the internal iliac arteries, and forming the posterior margin of the ovarian fossae. In this part of their course they lie internal to the superior vesical vessels, the obturator nerve, artery and vein, and the inferior vesical vessels.

The ureters then turn medially and forwards at the level of the ischial spines and run through the pelvic fascia above the upper surface of the levator ani muscles to the bladder. In this region they pass through the bases of the broad ligaments, special tunnels (the ureteric canals) running through Mackenrodt's ligaments. Here they lie lateral to the cervix and close to the lateral fornices of the vagina; the uterine vessels on their way from the side walls of the pelvis cross over them.

In front of the cervix the ureters enter the bladder. They run obliquely for about 19mm through the bladder wall, this device serving as a mechanism whereby urinary regurgitation from the bladder into the ureters is prevented. Finally they open into the cavity of the bladder at the posterior lateral angles of the trigone.

The blood supply in the pelvic part of their course is from the common iliac, the internal iliac, the uterine and the vesical arteries, and returns via corresponding veins.

The lymph drainage is to the internal, external and common iliac lymph nodes.

The nerve supply is from the aortic, renal and superior and inferior hypogastric plexuses.


## THE BLADDER

The bladder is a hollow muscular distensible organ, lying in the true pelvis, which acts as a reservoir for the storage of urine prior to micturition. It is roughly pyramidal in shape when empty, having a base or trigone which rests on the vagina, and an upper surface, continuous with the floor of the utero-vesical pouch, which extends from the cervix to the upper border of the symphysis pubis. The anterior part of the upper surface is sometimes termed the apex of the bladder. It has two infero-lateral surfaces which rest on the upper surface of the levator ani muscles.

The trigone of the bladder is triangular in shape, with its base placed behind and its apex in front (Fig. 2/7). Each of its three sides measures about 2.5cm. At the extremities of the base are placed the ureteric orifices—these are narrow slit-like apertures, through which the ureters open after having obliquely penetrated the bladder wall. The apex of the trigone is formed by the internal meatus where the urethra leaves the bladder. This region is known as the bladder neck.

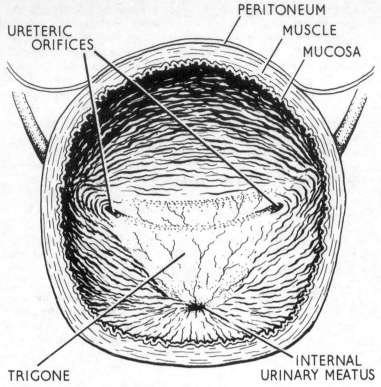

**Fig. 2/7:**   Dissection of the bladder

The normal capacity of the bladder is about 500ml although under pathological conditions it may contain many litres of urine when its shape becomes more globular, and its upper part rises into the abdomen.

**Structure**
The bladder walls are formed by the following layers:
   1. The cavity is lined by transitional epithelium which rests on a layer of areolar tissue. The epithelium is thrown into folds or rugae, similar to those of the vaginal walls, to allow for distension; this arrangement however is absent over the trigone, where the epithelium is firmly bound down to the subjacent muscle.
   2. The epithelium of the bladder is surrounded by three coats of smooth muscle, which are arranged as inner longitudinal, middle

circular and outer longitudinal layers. This muscle is known as the detrusor muscle, and is so called because when it contracts it expels the urine from the bladder during the act of micturition. The circular muscle is thickened around the internal meatus to form the internal sphincter of the bladder. It is in a constant state of contraction except during micturition.

The muscles in the trigone of the bladder have a rather special arrangement. The muscle fibres running between the ureteric orifices are collected into a band which is known as the interureteric ridge. The muscle fibres between the urethral orifice and the ureteric orifices may also be raised into similar ridges.

3. The upper surface of the bladder is covered with peritoneum, while its remaining surfaces are invested with visceral pelvic fascia.

### The Ligaments of the Bladder

Five ligaments are attached to the bladder.

*A fibrous band* known as the urachus runs from the apex of the bladder up the anterior abdominal wall to the umbilicus. During fetal life this structure is patent when it passes through the umbilicus into the umbilical cord and constitutes the allantois.

*Two fibrous ligaments* pass from the sides of the bladder to the side walls of the pelvis. These are called the lateral ligaments of the bladder.

*Two ligaments, the pubo-vesical ligaments,* attach the neck of the bladder anteriorly to the pubic bones. These are weak structures and form part of the pubo-cervical ligaments.

### Relations

*Anterior.* The pubic bones, separated from the bladder by a space filled with fatty tissue—this is known as the Cave of Retzius.

*Posterior.* The cervix, with the ureters on either side entering the lateral angles of the trigone.

*Lateral.* The lateral ligaments of the bladder and the side walls of the pelvis.

*Superior.* The body of the anteverted uterus and the intestines lying in the utero-vesical pouch.

*Inferior.* The upper half of the anterior vaginal wall lying below the trigone, and the levator ani muscles situated below the infero-lateral surfaces.

The blood supply is from the superior and inferior vesical arteries, with a few twigs from the uterine and vaginal arteries. The veins drain into corresponding vessels.

The lymph drainage is into the external iliac glands and obturator glands.

The nerve supply is from the sympathetic and para-sympathetic systems.

## THE URETHRA

The urethra is a narrow tube 3.5cm in length, which passes from the internal meatus of the bladder to open into the vestibule.

### Course
It runs practically embedded in the lower half of the anterior vaginal wall. At its origin from the bladder it is surrounded by a thickening of the circular muscle of the bladder which functions as an internal sphincter. It then passes between the two levator ani muscles, and below these it is enclosed by bands of striated muscle, known as the membranous sphincter of the urethra, which although it is not a true external sphincter, functions in that capacity.

### Structure
The wall of the urethra contains the following layers:
  1. The lumen is lined by transitional epithelium in its upper half and squamous epithelium in its lower half.
  2. These epithelia rest on a layer of vascular connective tissue.
  3. An inner longitudinal coat of smooth muscle. These muscle fibres are continuous with the inner longitudinal fibres of the bladder, which pass through the internal meatus.
  4. An outer circular coat of smooth muscle fibres.

The lumen of the urethra is normally closed, when its wall is thrown into small longitudinal folds. Several minute diverticula or crypts open into the urethra. These run longitudinally in the urethral wall for a short distance and communicate with the lumen of the urethra at their lowest point. The two largest of these are Skene's tubules which open on to the surface just lateral to the urethral orifice in the vestibule. They correspond to the prostate gland in the male.

The blood supply is from the inferior vesical and pudendal arteries. The veins drain similarly.

The lymph drainage is into the internal iliac glands.

The internal sphincter is supplied by the sympathetic, while the membranous sphincter is under voluntary control via the pudendal nerve.

**The Physiology of Micturition**

When the bladder is filled with about 300ml of urine, sensations are conveyed to the hypothalamus and cortical centres of the brain through sensory sympathetic nerves, informing the patient that the performance of micturition is necessary. This act can be voluntarily postponed until a suitable moment, although contractions occur in the bladder wall which render the desire for micturition practically irresistible when the volume of urine reaches 700ml.

When the act of micturition is performed nerve impulses from the cerebral cortex increase the para-sympathetic activity and decrease the sympathetic activity causing relaxation of the internal sphincter and contraction of the bladder muscle. The external sphincter is relaxed, intra-abdominal pressure is raised and expulsion of urine takes place.

## THE RECTUM

The rectum is the continuation of the pelvic colon. It begins at the level of the third sacral vertebra, lies in the hollow of the sacrum and ends below at the tip of the coccyx, where it makes a right-angled bend backwards to join the anal canal. It is a distensible tube about 12.5cm in length and wider in its lower part where it forms the rectal ampulla. As it passes downwards it has three bends, two to the right and one to the left, which help to support the weight of the contained faeces. At these bends the mucous membrane forms prominent ridges which are sometimes called the valves of Houston. The rectum is attached to the pelvic wall by condensations of visceral pelvic fascia which form its lateral supporting ligaments.

### Structure

The rectal wall consists of the following coats:

1. The cavity is lined by columnar cells which dip down in places into the submucosa to form tubular glands.

2. A vascular submucous layer which lies below the surface epithelium.

3. An inner circular layer of smooth muscle.

4. An outer longitudinal layer of smooth muscle.

5. A peritoneal investment which differs at varying levels:
    (a) The upper third is covered by peritoneum in front and at the sides.
    (b) The middle third has a peritoneal lining only in front.

This peritoneal covering of the rectum forms the posterior wall of the pouch of Douglas.

(c) The lowest third has no peritoneal coat.

6. In the places where the peritoneum is absent the rectum is invested with a layer of visceral pelvic fascia.

## Relations

*Anterior*. The pouch of Douglas lies in front of the rectum above, while its lowest third is in direct relation with the middle third of the vagina.

*Posterior*. The sacrum and coccyx.

*Lateral*. The intestines in the pouch of Douglas. The lateral ligaments of the rectum pass from the lateral borders of the rectum to the pelvic walls, while the utero-sacral ligaments encircle the rectum as they pass from the uterus to the sacrum.

The blood supply is from the superior haemorrhoidal (the terminal branch of the inferior mesenteric artery) and the middle haemorrhoidal arteries (from the internal iliac arteries). The veins drain similarly.

The lymph drainage from the lower part of the rectum is into the sacral, the internal iliac and common iliac groups of glands. The upper part drains through vessels which accompany the superior haemorrhoidal vessels to the lymphatic glands lying in the pelvic mesocolon.

The nerve supply is formed by the sympathetic and para-sympathetic systems similar to other pelvic organs.

## THE ANAL CANAL

The anal canal is a short tube, about 2.5cm in length, passing from the point where the rectum makes a right-angled turn backwards opposite the tip of the coccyx to end in the anus. During its short course it passes between the levator ani muscles, which in fact encircle it and hold it with a sling-like action in its normal position.

## Structure

Although the anal canal is so short, it has a different structure in its upper and lower parts (Fig. 2/8):

1. In its upper two-thirds the anal canal is lined by mucous membrane similar to that of the rectum. This mucosa is not a flat surface but is raised into about six longitudinal folds—the columns of Morgagni. These columns contain veins, which if they become enlarged, may give rise to internal haemorrhoids. Sometimes these become so large that they prolapse through the anal orifice and become visible on inspection, a frequent occurrence during pregnancy and labour. The

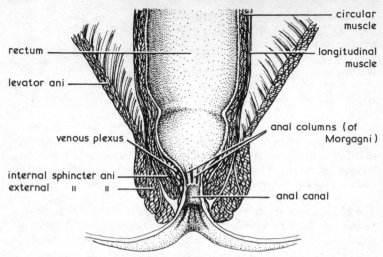

**Fig. 2/8:**   The structure of the anal canal

lowest ends of the columns are connected by small folds of mucosa which form the anal valves.

2. The lowest third of the anal canal is lined by squamous epithelium continuous with that of the normal skin. Its junction with the mucous membrane above is marked by a distinct white line.

3. The muscle coat of the anal canal is arranged in a special manner:

  (a) The circular muscle of the rectum is prolonged downwards to surround the anal canal where it becomes thickened to form the internal sphincter of the anus.

  (b) A second sphincter is formed by the external sphincter of the anus. This is a striated muscle, partly attached to the coccyx, which surrounds the anus and enters into the formation of the perineal body, thus belonging to the superficial perineal group of muscles.

  (c) The longitudinal muscle coat of the rectum joins with the levator ani muscles, which become attached to the anal wall between the two sphincters, where they form a supporting sling.

4. Sometimes small veins external to the anus become dilated and form external piles.

**Relations**

*Superior.* The rectum.

*Anterior.* The perineal body and the lowest third of the vagina.

*Posterior.* A mass of fibrous tissue lying between the anal canal and the coccyx, known as the ano-coccygeal body.

*Lateral.* The levator ani muscles, and lateral to them the ischio-rectal fossae. These are large pads of fatty tissue which lie between the anal canal and the lower part of the lateral pelvic walls.

The blood supply is received from the superior, middle and inferior haemorrhoidal arteries and the median sacral artery. The veins drain in a similar manner, those forming the superior haemorrhoidal vein being the site of origin of internal haemorrhoids.

The lymph drainage is into the internal iliac glands, the anus itself draining with the skin of the perineum into the inguinal glands.

The nerve supply of the upper half of the anus is via the autonomic plexuses, the lower half being supplied by the somatic inferior haemorrhoidal nerve.

### The Physiology of Defaecation

Defaecation is normally a voluntary act under the control of the will. When faeces enter the rectum from the pelvic colon by the action of peristalsis they give rise to the desire to defaecate. During the act the pelvic colon and rectum contract by para-sympathetic action, and increased intra-abdominal pressure expels the faeces. The anal canal, which is normally closed, opens through relaxation of the sphincters to allow the faeces to pass, and this expansion is permitted by the soft ischio-rectal fossae. At the end of the act the anus is raised by the levator ani muscles which surround the anal canal (hence their name), the sphincters become contracted, and the rectum is then closed to the exterior.

## THE PELVIC FLOOR

The soft tissues which fill the outlet of the pelvis comprise what is known as the pelvic floor. It is apparent that in the erect attitude which human beings have adopted, the weight of the abdominal contents rests on the floor of the pelvis, and in consequence this is a strong structure made up of fascia and muscles. At the same time, the pelvic outlet is the exit from the body whereby the contents of the bladder, uterus and rectum are evacuated; accordingly the pelvic floor is pierced by the urethra, vagina and anal canal.

### The Muscles of the Pelvic Floor

It is convenient first to consider the muscles which comprise the pelvic floor. They consist of two deep muscles, the levator ani, and a superficial group of muscles known as the superficial perineal muscles. The levator ani muscles and the pelvic fascia which clothes them above and below are sometimes referred to as the pelvic diaphragm.

### The Levator Ani Muscles

These are two powerful muscles, 3 to 5mm in thickness, lying on either side of the pelvis (Fig. 2/9). They arise from the circumference of the true pelvis and converge towards the midline, with a concave upper and convex lower surface, to be inserted into the perineal body, the anal canal, the ano-coccygeal body, the coccyx and the lower end of the sacrum. They consist of three parts, each one of which is associated with one of the constituent bones of the innominate bone:

*The pubo-coccygeus* arises from the back of the bodies of the pubic bones. The muscle fibres sweep posteriorly below the bladder, on either side of the urethra and the lowest third of the vagina, to enter the perineal body. Here some fibres cross from side to side and form the deep half of the perineal body: others pass on and are inserted into the wall of the anal canal, while others form a loop around this structure

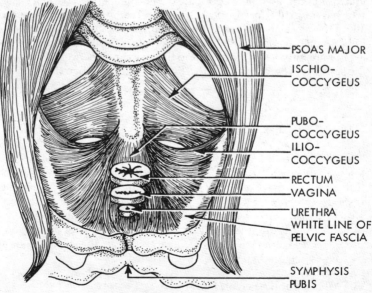

**Fig. 2/9:**   The pelvic floor musculature

known as the ano-rectal sling. The longest fibres gain insertions into the ano-coccygeal body and the coccyx.

*The ilio-coccygeus* takes origin from the iliac part of the pelvic brim in lower animals, but in human beings the origin is different and the muscle fibres arise from the fascia covering the obturator internus muscle. The site of origin of the ilio-coccygeus is marked by a thick white line, known as the 'white line of pelvic fascia'. The fibres sweep downwards and inwards and are inserted into the ano-coccygeal body and the coccyx.

*The ischio-coccygeus* is situated in front of the sacro-spinous ligament, and is sometimes referred to as a separate muscle, the coccygeus muscle. Its fibres arise behind the ilio-coccygeus from the spine of the ischium and pass downwards and inwards to be inserted into the coccyx and the lowest piece of the sacrum.

It can thus be understood that in the upright position the levator ani muscles form a hammock across the pelvis which carries the weight of the abdominal organs, and which is pierced by the urethra, vagina and anal canal (Fig. 2/10). A space exists behind the muscle corresponding to the position of the greater sciatic notch, which on account of the tilting of the pelvis when the patient stands erect, is really the posterior wall of the pelvis rather than its floor. This space is filled by the

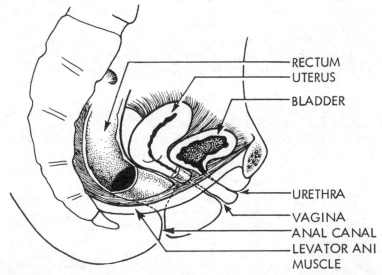

RECTUM
UTERUS
BLADDER
URETHRA
VAGINA
ANAL CANAL
LEVATOR ANI
MUSCLE

**Fig. 2/10:** Lateral view of the pelvis to show how the levator ani muscles form part of the pelvic floor

piriformis muscle which passes from the sacrum through the greater sciatic notch on its way to gain insertion into the greater trochanter of the femur. Nerves from the sacral plexus also leave the pelvis through the notch with the piriformis muscle.

The function of the levator ani muscles is to form a muscular diaphragm to support the pelvic viscera, and to counteract any increase in the intra-abdominal pressure. It thus supports the bladder and vagina, and constricts the lower end of this latter organ; when it contracts the ano-rectal sling pulls the rectum, at the point where it becomes continuous with the anal canal, towards the pubic bones and so kinks the gut. It also closes the anal canal, and lifts up the anus after defaecation thereby assisting in the expulsion of faeces. During labour it plays some part in guiding the fetus in its passage through the birth canal.

The attachment of the levator ani to the coccyx has already been noted. In lower animals where the coccyx forms the tail, the levator ani functions as a tail-moving muscle. Thus a happy dog wags his tail by alternately contracting his ischio-coccygei, while a naughty dog slinks away with his tail drawn down by his pubo-coccygei.

The levator ani muscle is supplied by the pudendal nerve and the fourth sacral nerve.

### The Superficial Perineal Muscles

These muscles lie in the pelvic outlet on the under surface of the anterior part of the levator ani muscles, forming the superficial half of the perineal body and surrounding the anal and vaginal orifices. On either side of the anal canal below the posterior part of the levator muscles lie the ischio-rectal fossae. The superficial perineal muscles are important as they are liable to injury during childbirth. They may be described as follows (Fig. 2/11):

*The external sphincter of the anus* surrounds the anal canal, lying below the internal sphincter and the levator ani. Anteriorly it enters into the formation of the perineal body, where it is attached to other superficial perineal muscles at a point known as the central point of the perineum. Posteriorly some of its fibres are attached to the tip of the coccyx. Its function is to close the lumen of the anal canal.

*The transverse perineal muscles* take origin from the ischial tuberosities and pass transversely inwards to meet their fellow of the opposite side and other perineal muscles in the central point of the perineum. They consist of superficial and deep portions—the deep muscle is enclosed between the layers of the triangular ligament. These muscles fix the position of the perineal body and help to support the lower part of the vagina.

*The bulbo-cavernosus* (or *bulbo-spongiosus*) *muscles* arise from the

SUPERFICIAL DISSECTION                                          DEEPER DISSECTION

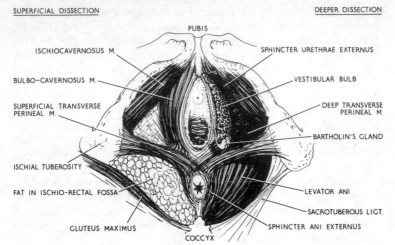

**Fig. 2/11:** Dissection of the perineum showing the superficial and deep muscles

central point of the perineum and pass forwards around the vagina, lying superficial to Bartholin's glands and the vestibular bulbs and deep to the labia. They are inserted into the corpora cavernosa of the clitoris in the upper part of the pubic arch. The action of these muscles is to diminish the size of the vaginal orifice and to cause engorgement of the clitoris, but they are small muscles and their action is weak.

*The ischio-cavernosus muscles* arise from the ischial tuberosities and pass upwards and inwards along the pubic arch to gain insertion into the corpora cavernosa of the clitoris. Their function is to cause engorgement of the clitoris.

*The membranous sphincter of the urethra.* Although from the obstetrical point of view this muscle is not situated in the perineum, it is anatomically allied to the other superficial perineal muscles. It lies between the layers of the triangular ligament. Its fibres arise from one pubic bone and pass above and below the urethra to the opposite pubic bone; as they do not encircle the urethra they do not constitute a true sphincter, but by their contraction they are able to occlude its lumen.

The superficial perineal muscles are supplied by the perineal branch of the pudendal nerve.

## The Triangular Ligament
This structure which is also known as the inferior fascia of the urogenital diaphragm and the perineal membrane is really the deep fascia

which invests these perineal muscles. It fills in the triangular space between the bulbo-cavernosus, ischio-cavernosus and transverse perineal muscles, and the deep transverse perineal muscles and the membranous sphincter of the urethra lie between its layers. It is pierced by the urethra and the vagina and helps to maintain them in their normal positions.

## The Perineal Body

The constituent parts of this structure have now been described. It is a fibro-muscular pyramid situated between the lowest third of the vagina in front, the anal canal behind and the ischial tuberosities laterally. Its deeper half consists of fibres from the levator ani which cross from side to side between the vagina and the anal canal, while its lower half is made up of the superficial perineal muscles. The centre of its lowest part, to which many of the superficial perineal muscles converge, is known as the central point of the perineum. It is covered by superficial fascia and skin.

A superficial perineal laceration occurring during childbirth may tear the skin and the bulbo-cavernosus and transverse perineal muscles; a deeper tear may involve the levator ani in addition, while a third degree tear lacerates the external sphincter of the anus. Damage to the membranous sphincter of the urethra during labour disturbs the support of the bladder neck, and leads to the development of stress incontinence.

## The Fascia of the Pelvic Floor

On the upper surface of the levator ani muscles are situated the bladder and ureters, the upper two-thirds of the vagina, the uterus with its appendages, and the rectum, together with the blood vessels, lymphatics and nerves which supply them. These organs are embedded in a layer of loose areolar tissue which invests them, fills the spaces between them, and extends from the pelvic peritoneum above to the levator ani muscles below. This is known as the pelvic fascia. It consists of two parts:

## The Parietal Pelvic Fascia

The pelvic wall is lined by a layer of this fascia, called the parietal pelvic fascia, part of which is thickened to form the 'white line of pelvic fascia', which gives origin to the ilio-coccygeal portion of the levator ani muscle. Below the levator ani it passes down the side wall of the pelvis and lines the lateral wall of the ischio-rectal fossa, while in front of this it fuses with the triangular ligament. Anteriorly, the parietal pelvic fascia covers part of the pubic bones, and posteriorly, it clothes the piriformis and is attached to the sacrum. Above, it is continuous with the fasciae of the abdominal wall.

## The Visceral Pelvic Fascia

The pelvic organs are invested by the visceral layer of pelvic fascia. The part of the fascia which surrounds the bladder and rectum is thickened to form the supporting ligaments of these organs, while the fascia investing the upper parts of the vagina and cervix contains muscle fibres and forms the supporting ligaments of the uterus as already described. This portion is sometimes called the parametrium. The fascia also lies between the two peritoneal layers which form the broad ligaments. As the ureters, vessels and nerves pass from the walls of the pelvis to the pelvic organs, they ramify in this layer of visceral pelvic fascia. It also covers the lower surface of the levator ani muscles, where it is known as the anal fascia.

The structures which form the pelvic floor from above downwards are thus (Fig. 2/12):

1. The pelvic peritoneum.
2. The visceral layer of pelvic fascia, condensed in places to form the supporting ligaments of the pelvic viscera.

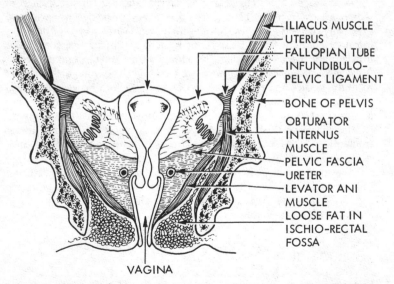

ILIACUS MUSCLE
UTERUS
FALLOPIAN TUBE
INFUNDIBULO-PELVIC LIGAMENT
BONE OF PELVIS
OBTURATOR INTERNUS MUSCLE
PELVIC FASCIA
URETER
LEVATOR ANI MUSCLE
LOOSE FAT IN ISCHIO-RECTAL FOSSA
VAGINA

**Fig. 2/12:** Coronal section of pelvis to show the formation of the pelvic floor. Note the relationship of the visceral pelvic fascia, the levator ani muscles and the ischio-rectal fossa

3. The levator ani muscles.
4. The anal fascia.
5. The superficial perineal muscles and the triangular ligament.
6. The superficial fascia and the ischio-rectal fossae.
7. The skin.

**Other Muscles of the Pelvis**

*The piriformis muscles.* These are two in number and occupy the posterior part of the pelvic wall. They arise from the anterior surface of the second, third and fourth sacral vertebrae, and pass out of the pelvis through the greater sciatic notch to be inserted into the greater trochanter of the femur. They are supplied by branches from the first and second sacral nerves, and their action is to rotate the thighs laterally.

*The obturator internus muscles.* These form part of the side walls of the pelvis and are covered by parietal pelvic fascia. They arise from the inner surfaces of the pubis, ischium, ilium and obturator membrane. The muscle fibres converge towards the lesser sciatic notch where they leave the pelvis to be inserted into the greater trochanter of the femur. Their nerve of supply is a branch from the sacral plexus and their function also is to rotate the thighs laterally.

*The iliacus muscles.* These are two flat triangular muscles, each of which arises from an iliac fossa. The fibres pass downwards and gradually converge as they lie over the pelvic brim and pass under the inguinal ligament. They are inserted into the tendon of the psoas major muscle. The iliacus is supplied by a branch from the femoral nerve.

*The psoas major muscles.* These are two muscles which arise mainly from the bodies and transverse processes of the lumbar vertebrae and pass downwards across the pelvic brim, below the inguinal ligament and in front of the hip joint, where they form a tendon. This is joined by the fibres of the iliacus muscle, and is inserted into the lesser trochanter of the femur. The nerve supply is received from the second, third, and fourth lumbar nerves.

These two muscles are sometimes considered to form a single functional unit known as the ilio-psoas muscle. Its function is to flex the thigh and, acting in conjunction with the gluteal muscles in the erect attitude, it helps to stabilise the hip joint.

## THE ARTERIES OF THE PELVIS

Four large arteries are responsible for the blood supply to the pelvic organs, namely the two ovarian arteries and the two internal iliac (or hypogastric) arteries. Also present are the fibrosed remains of two

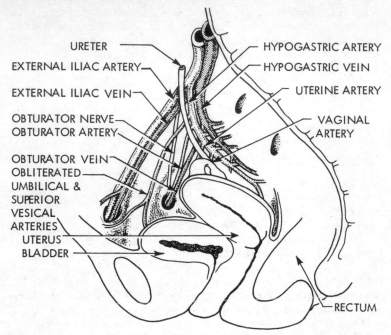

**Fig. 2/13:** Lateral view of the pelvis to show the arteries and veins

large arteries which function during fetal life—the obliterated hypo-gastric arteries (Fig. 2/13).

**The Ovarian Arteries**
These arise from the abdominal aorta, just below the level of the renal arteries.

*Course*
Each artery passes obliquely downwards and outwards behind the peritoneum and reaches the pelvic brim, where it crosses the external iliac artery and vein and enters the true pelvis. It then passes through the infundibulo-pelvic ligament, enters the broad ligament of the uterus and passes through the mesovarium into the ovary. One or more branches supply the Fallopian tube, while another passes down alongside the uterus to unite with the uterine artery of the same side.

**The Internal Iliac Arteries**
Each artery begins in front of the upper part of the sacro-iliac joint,

where the common iliac artery terminates by dividing into the external and internal iliac arteries. The external iliac vessel passes below the inguinal ligament and enters the thigh, being the main vessel of supply to the lower limb, while the internal iliac artery is the chief source of supply to all the pelvic viscera.

## Course
The internal iliac artery, which is only about 5cm long, passes downwards into the pelvis in front of the sacro-iliac joint to reach the upper part of the greater sciatic notch.

## Relations
During its course it has the following relations:

*Posterior.* The internal iliac vein, the lumbo-sacral nerve trunk and the sacro-iliac joint.

*Anterior.* The ureter and the ovarian fossa.

*Lateral.* The pelvic wall.

*Medial.* The pelvic peritoneum.

## Branches
Opposite the upper border of the sciatic notch the internal iliac artery divides into a large number of branches:

*The uterine artery* runs medially from the lateral pelvic wall in the visceral pelvic fascia on the upper surface of the levator ani muscle, crossing above the ureter by the side of the cervix, to reach the uterus at the level of the internal os. It then ascends alongside the corpus of the uterus, between the layers of the broad ligament, in a winding and tortuous manner. When it reaches the cornu it turns laterally and joins with a branch of the ovarian artery below the Fallopian tube. It gives off branches which supply the lower end of the ureter, the cervix and the vagina and sends numerous branches into the body of the uterus and the Fallopian tube. Those entering the myometrium pass in a circular direction towards the midline where they anastomose with those of the opposite side. They constitute the coronary arteries.

*The vaginal artery* passes medially in the visceral pelvic fascia to reach the vagina, which it supplies. It anastomoses with branches from the uterine arteries above, and sometimes forms large vessels which pass down the anterior and posterior vaginal walls in the midline. These are known as the azygos arteries of the vagina.

*The superior vesical artery* runs forwards to the bladder where it supplies its upper part.

*The inferior vesical artery* passes forwards to the base of the bladder, which it supplies along with the lower end of the ureter.

*The middle haemorrhoidal artery* passes medially to supply the rectum.

*The internal pudendal artery* leaves the pelvis through the greater sciatic notch, crosses the ischial spine and then enters the ischio-rectal fossa through the lesser sciatic notch. It then runs in a tunnel (Alcock's canal) in the parietal pelvic fascia in the lateral wall of the fossa above the ischial tuberosity, and passes along the pubic arch, supplying the anal canal (by a branch called the inferior haemorrhoidal artery), the perineal body, the labia, the vestibular bulbs and the clitoris. Throughout most of its course it is accompanied by the pudendal nerve.

Other branches are the obturator, superior and inferior gluteals, the ilio-lumbar and the lateral sacral arteries. These in the main are arteries which supply muscles outside the pelvis.

### The Obliterated Hypogastric Arteries

During fetal life, when the legs are relatively small, the major part of the fetal blood passes from the aorta and common iliac arteries into the internal iliac arteries, which carry it up the anterior abdominal wall to the umbilicus. During this time these arteries are known as the hypo-gastric arteries, and after passing through the umbilicus they enter the cord and become the umbilical arteries.

At birth, when the fetal circulation changes into that of the adult, modifications occur in the fetal hypogastric arteries (see Chapter 6). The proximal portions remain patent and become the superior vesical arteries; the distal portions are changed into fibrous ligaments, which are then known as the obliterated hypogastric arteries. These can be traced on each side of the pelvic wall as ligaments running from the superior vesical arteries on to the anterior abdominal wall outside the peritoneum. They then pass in a converging manner up to the umbili-cus, which they enter alongside the urachus.

### Branches from the Femoral Artery

The superficial and deep external pudendal branches of the femoral artery ascend from the upper part of the thigh and supply the labia majora.

## THE VEINS OF THE PELVIS

These are very similar in their distribution to the arteries which they accompany, the blood from the pelvic organs draining away chiefly by the ovarian and internal iliac veins.

## The Ovarian Veins

These are formed within the broad ligament by branches from the ovary, uterus and Fallopian tube which unite and form a plexus; this passes into the infundibulo-pelvic ligament, where it is called the pampiniform plexus. Finally a single ovarian vein is formed on each side which passes upwards behind the peritoneum and ends in a different manner on the two sides. On the right, the ovarian vein opens into the inferior vena cava below the renal veins, while on the left, the ovarian vein opens into the left renal vein itself.

## The Internal Iliac Veins

These are made up of tributaries which originate in large plexuses around the vagina, uterus, and bladder, and then unite to form veins which correspond to the branches of the internal iliac arteries. They pass up posterior to the internal iliac arteries, and join with the external iliac veins coming from the legs to form the common iliac veins. These unite to form the inferior vena cava.

## THE LYMPHATICS OF THE PELVIS

There are numerous groups of lymphatic glands which receive lymph from the pelvic organs and transmit it to further groups on its way to reach the cisterna chyli.

The most important groups are as follows (Fig. 2/14):

*The inguinal group* consists of a horizontal set lying along the inguinal ligament of the groin, and a vertical set passing for about 11.4cm down into the thigh alongside the saphenous and femoral veins. The former group drains the vulva, including Bartholin's gland, the anus, the lowest third of the vagina and the perineal body while the latter group receives lymph from the buttocks and lower limbs. A small lymphatic vessel from the fundus of the uterus passes along the round ligament to join the horizontal group of glands.

*The external iliac group* lies alongside the external iliac vessels and receives lymph from the inguinal glands in addition to directly draining the bladder.

*The parametrial gland* is only sometimes present, and then is placed in the parametrium alongside the cervix, close to where the uterine artery and vein cross the ureter. It drains lymph from the cervix.

*The obturator group* lies in the obturator fossa, in the upper part of the foramen ovale, and receives lymph from the cervix and bladder.

*The internal iliac group* is situated along the course of the internal iliac vessels, and receives lymph mainly from the body and cervix of the

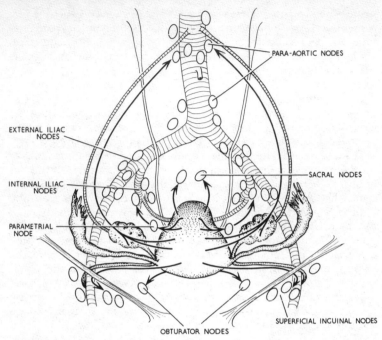

**Fig. 2/14:**  The lymphatic drainage of the pelvis

uterus, the upper two-thirds of the vagina, the urethra, the rectum and the anal canal. These glands also drain the parametrial and obturator glands.

*The sacral group* is placed lateral to the rectum in the hollow of the sacrum, and receives lymph from the uterus, upper vagina and rectum.

*The common iliac glands* surround the common iliac vessels, and receive lymph from the internal and external iliac groups and the sacral group.

*The lumbar glands* directly drain the ovaries and Fallopian tubes, and also receive lymph from the common iliac glands before transmitting it to the cisterna chyli.

## THE NERVES OF THE PELVIS

The pelvic organs are supplied by two sets of nerves, the sympathetic and para-sympathetic systems, whose functions are mutually antagonistic. The sympathetic nerves inhibit muscles which expel visceral contents, cause sphincters to contract and vessels to undergo constriction. The para-sympathetic fibres have the opposite effect and cause visceral organs to expel their contents, sphincters to relax, and vessels to become dilated.

### The Sympathetic Supply
The sympathetic supply in the main is the pelvic continuation of the large abdominal sympathetic plexuses, the most important of which are the coeliac or solar plexus, the aortic plexus and the renal plexuses.

The aortic plexus is continued below the level of the bifurcation of the aorta as a large network of nerves which lies in front of the last lumbar vertebra and the promontory of the sacrum. This is sometimes called the 'pre-sacral nerve', and it is joined by branches from the lumbar sympathetic chains. As it passes downwards it divides into two branches which terminate in plexuses lying in the floor of the pouch of Douglas on each side of the rectum, in the region of the utero-sacral ligaments. This network also receives fibres from the para-sympathetic system. From here nerves pass to all the pelvic viscera.

The ovarian plexus consists of sympathetic fibres derived from the renal and coeliac plexuses which accompany the ovarian vessels through the infundibulo-pelvic ligaments to supply the ovaries and the Fallopian tubes.

### The Para-Sympathetic Supply
The para-sympathetic nerves are known as the nervi erigentes, and are derived from the second and third sacral segments. The fibres emerge from the anterior sacral foramina corresponding to these segments of the cord and subsequently are distributed to all the pelvic viscera.

### Somatic Nerves
Many of the nerves which supply the lower limbs pass through the pelvis to reach their destinations. Large nerve trunks emerge through the four anterior sacral foramina on each side, and divide and unite to form the sacral plexus. This lies on the posterior wall of the pelvic cavity in front of the piriformis muscle, and is joined from above by the lumbo-sacral nerve trunk (derived from the fourth and fifth lumbar nerves) which passes in front of the sacro-iliac joint to reach it. The terminal branches of the plexus leave the pelvis through the greater sciatic notch in company with the piriformis muscle behind the posterior part of the levator ani.

Some of these nerves are of importance to obstetricians:

*The pudendal nerve* which is a branch of the sacral plexus leaves the pelvis through the greater sciatic notch, crosses the ischial spine and re-enters the pelvis through the lesser sciatic notch to pass into Alcock's canal in the lateral wall of the ischio-rectal fossa above the ischial tuberosity. It then gives off the inferior haemorrhoidal nerve which supplies the anal canal and its sphincters. Its terminal branches, the perineal nerve and the dorsal nerve of the clitoris, then run along the pubic arch and supply the superficial perineal muscles, the lower part of the levator ani and the skin of the vulva. The internal pudendal vessels accompany this nerve and its branches throughout their course.

Regional anaesthesia may be induced for forceps delivery or breech delivery by injecting a local anaesthetic solution into Alcock's canal. This causes anaesthesia of the vulva, lower vagina and perineum, which are supplied by sensory branches from the pudendal nerve. Complete anaesthesia, however, is only achieved if three other nerves which supply the skin of the vulva are also infiltrated with the solution. These are:

1. The ilio-inguinal nerve, which emerges from the inguinal canal with the round ligament of the uterus and supplies the skin of the anterior part of the vulva.

2. The genital branch of the genito-femoral nerve, whose course and distribution are similar.

3. The perineal branch of the posterior cutaneous nerve of the thigh, which supplies the skin of the posterior part of the vulva.

*A branch from the fourth sacral nerve* passes directly to supply the upper part of the levator ani muscles and part of the external anal sphincter.

*The lumbo-sacral trunk* may be injured during difficult labours, as it lies in front of the sacro-iliac joint. The peroneal and anterior tibial muscles which are supplied by this nerve trunk in the leg may then be paralysed, giving rise to the condition known as foot-drop. This is rarely seen in modern obstetrics.

# Chapter Three

# The Anatomy of the Bony Pelvis

A knowledge of the bony pelvis is of great importance to the student of midwifery, for during birth the fetus has to traverse the relatively unyielding ring which it forms on its passage from the uterus to the vulva. It is composed of the two innominate bones, which comprise its anterior and lateral parts, together with the sacrum and coccyx, which are placed posteriorly. Each innominate bone is formed by the fusion of three bones, the ilium, ischium and pubis (Figs. 3/1 and 3/2).

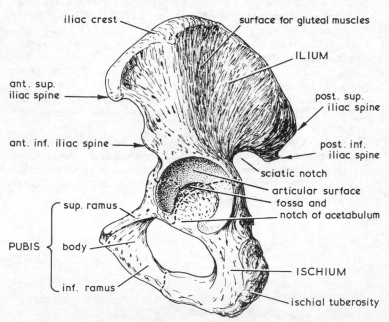

**Fig. 3/1:** The external surface of the left innominate bone (Dotted lines indicate the limits of the component parts)

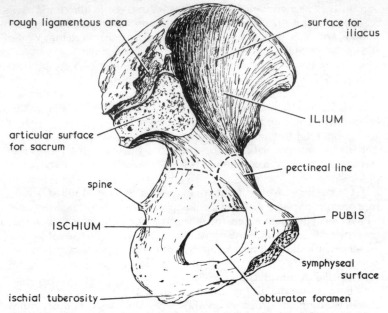

rough ligamentous area

surface for
iliacus

ILIUM

articular surface
for sacrum

pectineal line

spine

PUBIS

ISCHIUM

symphyseal
surface

ischial tuberosity

obturator foramen

**Fig. 3/2:** The internal surface of the left innominate bone (Dotted lines
indicate the limits of the component parts)

## THE BONES OF THE PELVIS

### The Ilium
This is made up of a relatively flat plate of bone above, and part of the
acetabulum below. It has the following characteristics:

1. The external aspect of the bony plate is gently curved and has a
roughened surface to which are attached the gluteal muscles of the
buttock.

2. The greater part of the inner aspect is smooth and concave,
forming the iliac fossa. In life a muscle originates from here, the iliacus,
which forms a soft platform on which the abdominal viscera rest.

3. The ridge which surmounts these two surfaces is known as the
iliac crest. This is shaped like an elongated letter S, and serves for the
attachment of the muscles of the abdominal wall. Anteriorly the crest
ends in the anterior superior iliac spine, a bony prominence which can
readily be palpated under the skin, while posteriorly it ends in the
posterior superior iliac spine, a point which is marked in the living
subject by a dimple at the level of the second sacral vertebra.

If the back be inspected these dimples will be seen to form the lateral angles of a flat diamond-shaped area, the upper point of which corresponds approximately to the spine of the fifth lumbar vertebra, while the lowest point lies in the upper end of the gluteal cleft.

4. Below the anterior superior iliac spine is another bony prominence, the anterior inferior iliac spine, while posteriorly is similarly situated the posterior inferior iliac spine.

5. At its lowermost part the ilium forms two-fifths of the acetabulum, where it fuses with the ischium and pubis.

6. Behind the acetabulum, the ilium forms the upper part of a large notch, the greater sciatic notch, through which pass the piriformis muscle and the nerves of the sacral plexus, on their way from the front of the sacrum into the thigh.

7. On the inner aspect of the bone, the iliac fossa is bounded below by a prominent ridge, which is the iliac part of the ilio-pectineal line. At a lower level the ilium enters into the formation of the side wall of the true pelvis, where it forms part of the floor of the acetabulum. Anteriorly the ilio-pectineal line swells into a bony prominence, at the point where the ilium fuses with the superior ramus of the pubis, to form the ilio-pectineal eminence.

8. Posterior to the ilio-pectineal line, and above the greater sciatic notch, is a roughened area where the ilium articulates with the sacrum to form the sacro-iliac joint. The tough supporting ligaments of this joint are attached to the bone behind the articular surface.

## The Ischium

The ischium is the lowest of the constituent bones of the innominate bone, and is formed by the following parts:

1. The head forms the lowest two-fifths of the acetabulum, where it fuses with the ilium and pubis.

2. Below the acetabulum a thick buttress of bone passes downwards and terminates in the ischial tuberosity. It is this part of the pelvis on which the weight of the body rests when sitting; it gives origin to the hamstring muscles of the thigh and is covered by a large bursa.

3. Passing upwards and inwards from the ischial tuberosity a small shaft of the ischium becomes continuous with the inferior ramus of the pubis, so forming the pubic arch.

4. The ischium thus forms the lower boundary of a large foramen, the obturator foramen or foramen ovale.

5. On its internal aspect the ischium forms the side wall of the true pelvis. Protruding inwards from its posterior edge, about 5cm above the tuberosity, is a conspicuous projection known as the ischial spine. This separates the greater sciatic notch above, which transmits the

piriformis muscle and the branches of the sacral plexus, from the lesser sciatic notch below, through which the tendon of the obturator internus muscle leaves the pelvis on its way to find insertion into the greater trochanter of the femur. The lesser notch is thus situated between the ischial spine above and the ischial tuberosity below.

## The Pubis

This is the smallest of the three bones forming the innominate bone and it is the only one which articulates with its fellow of the opposite side. Each pubic bone presents the following features:

1. The body of the pubis is square-shaped, with its medial side entering with that of its fellow into the formation of a joint known as the symphysis pubis.

2. The upper surface of the body forms a crest, the pubic crest, which ends laterally in the pubic tubercle.

3. Laterally the superior ramus passes to the acetabulum, of which it forms one-fifth, where it fuses with the ilium and ischium. Its junction with the ilium passes through the ilio-pectineal eminence. Its upper surface is marked by a ridge which runs from the pubic tubercle to the ilio-pectineal eminence. This is the forward extension of the ilio-pectineal line on to the pubis and is known as the pubic part of the ilio-pectineal line. The superior ramus completes the upper boundary of the foramen ovale.

4. Below the body of the pubis, the inferior ramus passes downwards and outwards to join the ischium, so forming the upper part of the pubic arch.

These three bones are each formed from pre-existing cartilage, and their separate ossification centres become fused together about the age of puberty. Ossification in the pelvis, however, is not completed before the age of twenty-five.

## The Sacrum

The sacrum is situated in the posterior part of the pelvis, where it articulates with the iliac portions of the two innominate bones at the sacro-iliac joints. It presents the following salient features (Fig. 3/3):

1. It consists usually of five sacral vertebrae which have become fused into one solid mass of bone. The anterior surface is smooth, and is concave from above downwards and slightly so from side to side, forming what is known as the hollow of the sacrum.

2. The first sacral vertebra overhangs the sacral hollow, and the central point of its upper projecting margin is known as the promontory of the sacrum.

3. The anterior branches of the first four pairs of sacral nerves

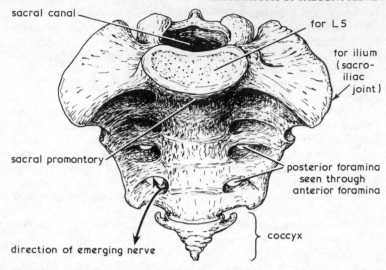

**Fig. 3/3:**    Anterior view of the sacrum and coccyx

emerge from the sacral canal through eight large foramina situated in the hollow of the sacrum. After forming the sacral plexus these nerves mostly pass through the greater sciatic notch into the thigh.

4. The posterior surface of the sacrum is rough and irregular and serves for the attachment of the ligaments and muscles of the back. Eight small foramina are present, through which the small posterior branches of the sacral nerves emerge to supply the skin of the buttocks and the muscles of the lower part of the back.

5. Passing longitudinally through the centre of the bone, but nearer to its posterior surface, is the sacral canal. This contains the sacral and coccygeal nerves derived from the spinal cord.

6. The sacral canal opens on to the posterior surface of the bone opposite the fifth sacral vertebra, between two projections known as the sacral cornua. If a caudal block is induced during labour, the local anaesthetic solution is injected between these two sacral cornua into the lower part of the sacral canal. The dura mater terminates opposite the second sacral vertebra, and the anaesthetic paralyses the nerves lying in the sacral canal below this level.

7. On its upper surface is a smooth oval area where the sacrum articulates with the fifth lumbar vertebra forming the lumbo-sacral joint. The lateral masses of bone on either side of this articular surface are known as the wings of the sacrum, or the sacral alae.

8. Opposite the first two sacral vertebrae the lateral aspects of the bone are relatively smooth where they enter into the formation of the sacro-iliac joints.

9. The lower margin of the sacrum forms a small smooth surface where it articulates with the coccyx at the sacro-coccygeal joint.

## The Coccyx

This small bone consists of four fused coccygeal vertebrae. It is triangular in shape with its base uppermost.

1. The first coccygeal vertebra articulates with the lower end of the sacrum at the sacro-coccygeal joint. It contains two small cornua which project upwards towards the sacral cornua.

2. The remaining three vertebrae are mere rudimentary nodules of bone; they are smooth on their inner surface where they support the rectum, while to their lowermost tip are attached the external anal sphincter and the ano-coccygeal body.


## THE PELVIC JOINTS

These are four in number, the two sacro-iliac joints, the symphysis pubis and the sacro-coccygeal joint.

## The Sacro-Iliac Joints

These articulations have the customary formation of joints with articular surfaces covered with cartilage on the articulating bones, a joint cavity filled with synovial fluid, a capsule lined by synovial membrane, and surrounding tough supporting ligaments. Their main features are as follows:

1.  The articular surfaces are placed
    (a) on the inner surface of the ilium above the greater sciatic notch, and
    (b) on the lateral aspect of the sacrum, extending for the length of the first two sacral vertebrae.
2.  The joint cavity is very small.
3.  The supporting ligaments pass from the sacrum and the fifth lumbar vertebra to the ilium both anterior and posterior to the joint cavity. The posterior ligaments are especially strong as they transmit the weight of the trunk, head and arms to the legs.

Movements at these joints occur under normal conditions but are very slight. They increase in range during pregnancy and labour when the ligaments become softened under the influence of the hormone relaxin.

**The Symphysis Pubis**

This joint consists of an oval disc of fibro-cartilage, about 3.8cm long, which is interposed between the bodies of the two pubic bones. It sometimes contains a small cavity, which is not lined by synovial membrane.

The symphysis is reinforced by supporting ligaments which pass from one pubic bone to the other in front, behind, above and below the disc of cartilage.

**The Sacro-Coccygeal Joint**

This small joint is situated between the lower border of the sacrum and the upper border of the coccyx. The articular surfaces of the bones are smooth and an intervertebral disc of cartilage lies between them, with supporting ligaments placed in front, behind and laterally. Sometimes a small joint cavity lined with synovial membrane is present.

Slight backward and forward movements of the coccyx on the lower end of the sacrum occur normally; the backward movement is greatly increased during labour at the time of the actual birth of the head.


THE PELVIC LIGAMENTS

The pelvic ligaments of importance to the midwife are as follows:

*The supporting ligaments of the pelvic joints* already described.

*The sacro-tuberous ligament,* which is a strong ligament passing from the posterior superior iliac spine and the lateral borders of the sacrum and the coccyx to the ischial tuberosity. It bridges across the greater and lesser sciatic notches.

*The sacro-spinous ligament,* which is another strong ligament passing from the side of the sacrum and coccyx across the greater sciatic notch to the ischial spine. It lies in front of the sacro-tuberous ligament.

*The inguinal ligament* (Poupart's ligament), which consists of the lower border of the tendon of the external oblique muscle of the anterior abdominal wall. It runs from the anterior superior iliac spine to the pubic tubercle forming the groin.


THE PELVIS AS A WHOLE

Although it is valuable to possess a knowledge of the constituent bones and joints of the pelvis (Fig. 3/4), it is more important to understand the pelvis as a whole, and to appreciate the manner in which it allows the fetal head to pass through during the process of labour.

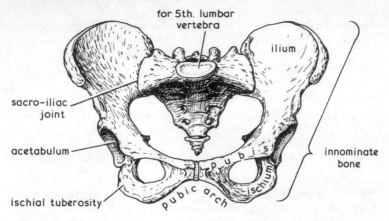

**Fig. 3/4:** The female pelvis

Consideration must therefore be given to the different regions of the pelvis, irrespective of individual bones, joints and ligaments.

## THE REGIONS OF THE PELVIS

### The Pelvic Brim

It is most important first of all to recognise the structures which comprise the brim of the pelvis. If a finger is placed on the promontory of the sacrum in a model pelvis and is passed around the brim, it will be found to touch the following structures in the order quoted:

The promontory of the sacrum.

The wing of the sacrum.

The upper part of the sacro-iliac joint.

The ilio-pectineal line.

The ilio-pectineal eminence.

The inner and upper border of the superior ramus of the pubis.

The inner and upper border of the body of the pubis.

The inner and upper border of the symphysis pubis.

The brim of the pelvis, traced in this way on both sides, forms a more or less oval area which divides the pelvis into two portions:

*The false pelvis,* which lies above the pelvic brim and consists mainly of the iliac fossae. This is of little importance in midwifery.

*The true pelvis,* which lies below the level of the pelvic brim. This is of great importance, and must be studied in detail.

**The True Pelvis**
The true pelvis is separated from the false pelvis by the pelvic brim. It
consists of three constituent parts:
1. The inlet or brim of the pelvis.
2. The cavity of the pelvis.
3. The outlet of the pelvis.

*The Inlet or Brim of the Pelvis*
The boundaries of this structure are described above. In the normal
female gynaecoid pelvis it is approximately oval in shape and is a flat
surface which could be occupied by a flat sheet of paper cut to the
appropriate shape. This flat surface is known as the plane of the brim.

*The Cavity of the Pelvis*
This extends from the inlet above to the outlet below. Its walls are
composed of the following structures:
1. The anterior wall consists of the posterior surfaces of the pubic
symphysis and pubic bones. It is 4.5cm deep.

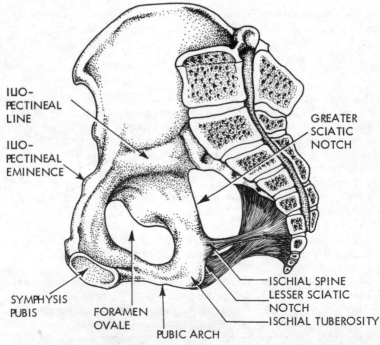

**Fig. 3/5:**  Section through the pelvis to show the formation of the lateral wall

2. The posterior wall is formed by the hollow of the sacrum. It is 12cm deep.

3. The lateral walls comprise the greater sciatic notch, the internal surface of a small portion of the ilium, the body of the ischium and the foramen ovale (Fig. 3/5). It is largely covered in life by the obturator internus muscle.

It will thus be seen that the cavity is curved in shape, the posterior wall being three times as long as the anterior wall. An imaginary surface is taken which extends from the mid-point of the symphysis in front to the junction of the second and third sacral vertebrae behind—this is known as the plane of the cavity of the pelvis.

## The Outlet of the Pelvis

Two outlets of the pelvis are described, the anatomical and the obstetrical.

*The anatomical outlet* is formed by the structures which mark the lower border of the pelvis (Fig. 3/6). Tracing them around the pelvis they are as follows:

The lower border of the pubic symphysis.

The pubic arch.

The inner border of the ischial tuberosity.

The sacro-tuberous ligament.

The tip of the coccyx.

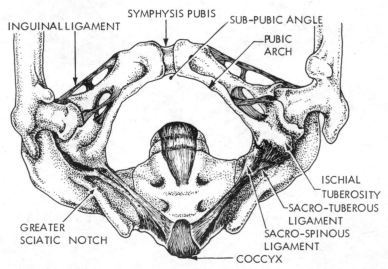

**Fig. 3/6:** The anatomical outlet of the pelvis, from above

To the obstetrician and the midwife this outlet has certain practical disadvantages. Thus it does not form a flat surface but one which rises and falls as it is traced around the periphery; also its size during labour is variable, depending upon the range of backward movement of the coccyx that occurs at this time.

*The obstetrical outlet* is the constricted lower portion of the pelvis and not merely its lower bony border (Fig. 3/7). It is a segment of the pelvis which lies between the anatomical outlet below and an artificial line above. The structures which mark this line are:

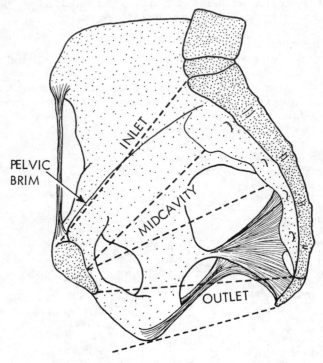

**Fig. 3/7:**   The obstetrical outlet of the pelvis

1. The lower border of the pubic symphysis.
2. A line passing obliquely across the pubis, foramen ovale and ischium to the ischial spine.
3. The sacro-spinous ligament.
4. The lower border of the sacrum.

The upper surface of the obstetrical outlet which is demarcated by this line, is a flat surface known as the plane of the outlet (Fig. 3/9). It is nearly constant in size during labour, being independent of the movements of the coccyx, and is the narrowest part of the pelvis. It is sometimes known as the narrow pelvic strait. The obstetrical outlet is thus a segment of the pelvis, lying between the plane of the outlet (or the narrow pelvic strait) above and the anatomical outlet below, and it is occupied in life by the muscles which form the pelvic floor.

## THE DIMENSIONS OF THE NORMAL PELVIS

Certain measurements are taken of the planes of the brim, cavity and outlet (Figs. 3/8 and 3/9). They are often referred to as diameters, but as they do not pass through the exact centres of the planes this is inaccurate.

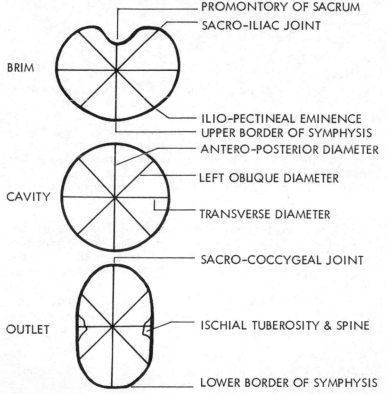

**Fig. 3/8:** The diameters of the pelvis

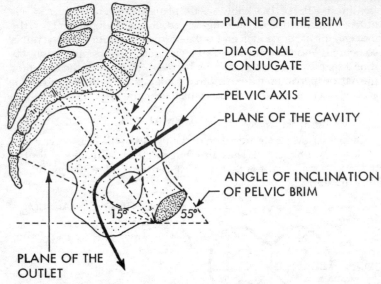

**Fig. 3/9:**   Diagram of the pelvis to show its three planes and the pelvic axis

### The Measurements of the Brim

1. A line passing from the centre of the promontory of the sacrum to the upper border of the pubic symphysis is known as the true conjugate of the pelvis, the conjugata vera, or the internal conjugate. The measurement from the promontory of the sacrum to the innermost margin of the symphysis is the obstetrical true conjugate and is what is referred to as the antero-posterior diameter of the brim. It measures 12.0cm in the European pelvis.

2. A line passing between the points farthermost apart on the ilio-pectineal lines constitutes the transverse diameter of the pelvic brim. It measures 13cm. The available transverse diameter of the brim is the width of the pelvis at the mid-point of the antero-posterior diameter and measures 12.5cm.

3. The oblique diameters pass from the sacro-iliac joints to the opposite ilio-pectineal eminences. The right oblique passes from the right joint, and the left from the left joint. They both measure 12.0cm in length.

4. Another measurement sometimes described is the sacro-cotyloid diameter. This is a line passing from the promontory of the sacrum to the ilio-pectineal eminence. It measures 9.5cm on each side.

The inlet is thus an oval structure, which is made heart-shaped by the projecting promontory, with its narrowest diameter running antero-posteriorly and its greatest diameter transversely.

It is impossible to measure the true conjugate directly during life by clinical examination, and it is found indirectly by first measuring the diagonal conjugate. This line, which can be estimated on vaginal examination, passes from the lower border of the pubic symphysis to the promontory of the sacrum. It measures 1.5cm more than the true conjugate. In practice it is impossible to reach the promontory of the sacrum on clinical examination of a normal pelvis so that the diagonal conjugate diameter is a theoretical measurement only.

**The Measurements of the Cavity**

1. The antero-posterior diameter passes from the mid-point of the symphysis to the junction of the second and third sacral vertebrae. It measures 12cm.

2. The transverse diameter passes in the plane of the cavity between the points farthermost apart in the lateral pelvic walls. It measures 12cm.

3. The oblique diameters pass obliquely in the plane of the cavity parallel to the oblique diameters of the brim. They each measure 12cm.

The plane of the cavity is thus circular in shape, with all diameters 12cm in length.

**The Measurements of the Outlet**

1. The antero-posterior diameter passes in the plane of the outlet from the lower border of the pubic symphysis to the lower border of the sacrum. It measures 12.5cm.

2. There are two transverse diameters:
   (i) The first is a line passing in the plane of the outlet between the two ischial spines. It measures 10.5cm.
   (ii) The second is a line passing between the inner borders of the two ischial tuberosities. It also measures 10.5cm.

Of the two, the former is usually slightly the smaller and therefore of more value in midwifery; the latter however is more easy to measure clinically.

3. The oblique diameters pass obliquely in a corresponding manner to the other oblique diameters, and are of little importance. They each measure 12.0cm.

The plane of the outlet is thus oval or diamond-shaped, with the longest diameter placed antero-posteriorly and the shortest transversely.

|        | Antero-posterior | Oblique | Transverse |
|--------|------------------|---------|------------|
| Brim   | 12.0cm           | 12.0cm  | 13.0cm     |
| Cavity | 12.0cm           | 12.0cm  | 12.0cm     |
| Outlet | 12.5cm           | 12.0cm  | 10.5cm     |

The Diameters of the Normal Pelvis

**Significance of Pelvic Measurements**
The most important of all these pelvic measurements are the shortest, as they indicate whether the pelvis is large enough to allow the fetal head to pass through during labour. The smallest diameters are thus the antero-posterior (true conjugate) of the brim (12.0cm) and the transverse diameter of the outlet (10.5cm). The true conjugate is the most important of these because when it is too short to allow the head to pass, normal delivery is impossible and labour becomes obstructed. When the transverse diameters of the outlet are too short, normal delivery may still be possible if the antero-posterior diameter of the outlet is sufficiently long, for it then allows the head to pass behind the ischial spines rather than between them. Obstructed labour at the outlet occurs only when both the transverse and antero-posterior diameters of the outlet are shortened.

Contraction of the pelvis at the brim is more common than contraction at the outlet.

External measurements of the pelvis are too inaccurate and are now no longer used as methods of assessing pelvic size.

**The Axes of the Pelvis**
Imaginary lines which pass through the centres of the planes at right angles to them are known as the axes of the pelvis. Those most usually described are:

1. The axis of the brim, which corresponds to an imaginary line passing from the umbilicus to the coccyx.

2. The axis of the outlet, which corresponds to a perpendicular line dropped from the sacral promontory on to the plane of the outlet.

These lines indicate the direction in which the fetus must travel to pass through the plane; hence the fetus passes downwards and backwards to enter the pelvis, and downwards and forwards to emerge from it. This is a result of the inequality in lengths of the anterior and posterior pelvic walls.

3. The pelvic axis is described as an imaginary line which joins the mid-points of successive planes through the pelvis (Fig. 3/9). It marks the direction the fetus moves during birth, passing down the cavity as far as the ischial spines and then curving forwards.

## The Angles of the Pelvis

There are five angles in the pelvis whose importance should be appreciated:

*The angle of inclination of the pelvic brim* is the angle the plane of the brim makes with the horizontal in the erect position (Fig. 3/9). It is usually about 55°. The greater the angle the harder it is for the fetal head to engage.

*The angle of inclination of the outlet* is the angle the upper border of the obstetrical outlet makes with the horizontal. It amounts to 15°, and is of little significance.

*The subpubic angle* is the angle between the two pubic rami which form the pubic arch. In the normal female gynaecoid pelvis this measures about 90°.

*The angle* between the plane of the brim and the anterior surface of the fifth lumbar vertebra is about 135°.

*The sacral angle* is the angle between the plane of the brim and the anterior surface of the first sacral vertebra. It usually measures 90°. It indicates the dimensions of the cavity relative to the size of the brim, for if the angle is less than 90° the cavity is smaller than the brim, while if it exceeds 90° the cavity is larger.

## Variations in Pelvic Shape

The normal European female pelvis which has been described above is called a gynaecoid pelvis and, in summary, the ideal gynaecoid pelvis has the following features:

1. The brim is rounded with no undue projection of the sacral promontory. The antero-posterior diameter should measure 12.0cm and the transverse 13cm. In the erect position the plane of the brim makes an angle of 55° to the horizontal.

2. The cavity is shallow with straight sides and the ischial spines should not project unduly. The sacrum is smoothly concave and the sacro-sciatic notches wide with the sacro-spinous ligaments 3.5cm in length.

3. The pubic arch is rounded, the subpubic angle being nearly 90°. The inter-tuberous diameter should be nearly 10.5cm.

Variations from the gynaecoid pelvis are found in a considerable proportion of women (Fig. 3/10). These are best seen on X-ray examination when they may be classified into the following types:

### The android brim

A brim of this type possesses certain characteristics of the male pelvis, being wedge-shaped with the apex of the wedge in front. Posteriorly a straight sacrum and a flattened promontory form the hind-pelvis, laterally the ilio-pectineal lines are relatively straight, and anteriorly they meet at an angle to form a narrow fore-pelvis. The maximum transverse diameter crosses the true conjugate in its posterior third close to the sacrum, resulting in a shortened posterior sagittal segment. Although the diameters of the brim may be equal to those of the gynaecoid shape, yet the space available for the passage of the fetus is considerably reduced.

Sometimes the android brim is associated with a characteristic cavity and outlet, when the whole pelvis may be said to be an android pelvis. In this event, the sacrum tends to be relatively straight throughout its whole length, the bones are large and the ischial spines prominent. The greater sciatic notches are narrow and the sacro-spinous ligaments short, while the pubic angle measures less than a right angle. All the outlet measurements may be reduced and the pelvis then constitutes one type of funnel pelvis.

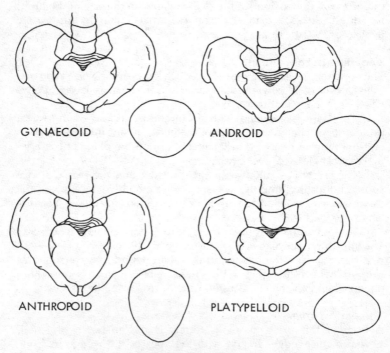

**Fig. 3/10:**  Variations in the shape of the pelvic brim

## The anthropoid brim

This type of brim has features similar to that of the anthropoid apes, and is characteristically long and narrow. It results from a reduction in the size of the maximum transverse diameter. Sometimes in fact the transverse diameter becomes equal to or smaller than the conjugate. It still, however, crosses the conjugate in its middle third, while the hind and fore-pelves are average in size or a little narrow.

When the whole pelvis is anthropoid in type certain distinctive features are present below the brim. The sacrum tends to be long and deeply concave, and it often contains six vertebrae (forming a high assimilation pelvis), while the greater sciatic notches are wide and the sacro-spinous ligaments long. The pubic angle is usually normal.

## The platypelloid brim

This type of brim is characteristically flattened, with the true conjugate reduced in size and the maximum transverse diameter elongated, so that there is at least 2.5cm difference between them.

When the platypelloid features involve the whole pelvis, reduced antero-posterior diameters and increased transverse diameters are present in the cavity and outlet, while the pubic angle may be wider than normal.

Many pelves, however, cannot be classified into these four types because they bear features characteristic of more than one group. When this occurs the hind and fore-pelves are allocated separately to the type to which they belong, and the brim is called andro-gynaecoid, or gynaeco-android, etc., as the case may be. The shape of the hind-pelvis is always stated first.

On some occasions abnormalities in the shape of the sacrum may occur, and a projecting convexity of bone may be seen on a lateral X-ray view at a level below the promontory. This is sometimes named a 'false promontory'. In this event the diameter of most importance is not the true conjugate but the smallest diameter passing from the symphysis to the nearest projecting point on the sacrum. This may be referred to as the 'effective conjugate', or 'available conjugate'.

In a pelvis with an android brim, the converging ilio-pectineal lines may make the fore-pelvis so narrow that the fetal head on its passage through the brim cannot approach close to the symphysis. In this case also the available conjugate is smaller than the true conjugate.

*Chapter Four*

# The Physiology of Menstruation

A full understanding of the phenomenon of menstruation requires knowledge first of the ovarian changes associated with ovulation, and secondly of the uterine changes preceding the actual blood flow. Ovulation is best understood by first considering the changes which affect the ovary in different age groups.

## THE OVARY AT DIFFERENT AGES

### In the Female Fetus and Young Girl

The ovary in a young female fetus is a solid organ, conforming to the anatomy already described in Chapter 1. On section the cortex and medulla of each ovary is found to contain about 200 000 primordial follicles. These consist of a large central cell, containing a prominent nucleus, which is enveloped by a single layer of small flattened cells called granulosa cells. Each of these central cells is an ovum which is capable in later life of becoming matured and fertilised and then developing into a baby; it can be seen from this that the female is lavishly endowed by nature with reproductive elements. The primordial follicles are separated from each other by the ovarian stroma—a connective tissue containing spindle cells—and are enclosed within the tunica albuginea and germinal epithelium.

When the fetus is 36 weeks old, changes begin in some of the primordial follicles and persist throughout infancy and early girlhood. These changes consist of an increase in the number of capsular cells, which become in consequence many layers thick around the ovum. This is followed by the appearance of fluid between the cells, known as the liquor folliculi. In this way some of the primordial follicles become converted into small cystic follicles, which are known as Graafian follicles.

### During Sexual Life

The Graafian follicles remain quite small until the girl reaches puberty, when she is about 13 to 14 years of age. After this they become much larger and some gradually attain a diameter of 8 to 12mm.

## Structure of a Graafian Follicle

The structures which comprise a Graafian follicle from within outwards are as follows (Figs. 4/1 and 4/2):

1. A large central cell, about 0.15mm in diameter, which is known as the ovum. It contains a large nucleus, with prominent nucleoli, and has many fat globules and particles scattered throughout its cytoplasm.

2. Immediately outside the ovum is a very narrow space, the perivitelline space.

3. Surrounding the ovum and the perivitelline space is a large clump of cells attached at one pole to the lining of the follicle. These cells are known as granulosa cells, and the clump they form around the ovum is called the discus proligerus or cumulus oophorus.

The cells of the discus next to the perivitelline space are arranged in such a manner that they appear to radiate from the ovum—this formation is called the corona radiata. These coronal cells contain amorphous material which forms a translucent membrane, the zona pellucida, lying immediately adjacent to the perivitelline space.

4. The follicle itself is lined with granulosa cells similar to those of the discus proligerus; these constitute the membrana granulosa or the zona granulosa. Scattered between the granulosa cells, especially near the discus proligerus prior to ovulation, are small globules of clear fluid surrounded by a ring of granulosa cells—these are sometimes known as Call-Exner bodies.

5. The follicle is filled with fluid—the liquor folliculi—which lies between the zona granulosa and the discus proligerus. It is probably formed by the granulosa cells.

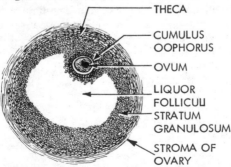

Fig. 4/1:   A Graafian follicle

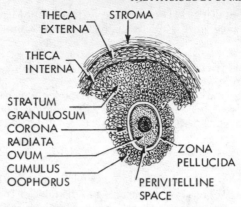

**Fig. 4/2:**  An enlarged view of the ovum and discus proligerus

6. Externally the membrana granulosa cells rest upon a basement membrane which encloses the whole follicle. This is called the membrana limitans externa or external limiting membrane.

7. Outside the follicle the stroma of the ovary is compressed to form a capsule, which is known as the theca. This is usually formed of two parts, an inner vascular layer known as the theca interna and an outer layer named the theca externa. These layers are more marked in lower animals than in human beings.

After ovulation has occurred the ovary also contains corpora lutea which are described later.

### The Post-Menopausal Ovary

Of the total number of primary follicles originally present in the ovaries only about 500 will mature during a woman's lifetime. The remainder are lost by degeneration. By the time of the menopause (46 to 50 years of age) all or most of the follicles will have been used up but postmenopausal ovaries have been found to contain a few follicles and this accounts for the occasional pregnancy occurring after the menopause. With increasing age the ovary becomes fibrous and greatly reduced in size.

## THE MECHANISM OF OVULATION

The reproductive phase of a woman's life begins at puberty and extends until menstruation ceases at the menopause. The onset of the first menstrual period is known as the menarche and usually occurs between the age of 10 and 16. During a reproductive lifetime one Graafian follicle each month outstrips its fellows and develops in size until it is about 16mm in diameter. It then protrudes from the surface of the ovary, with the discus proligerus and the contained ovum lying in its most projecting part. As it enlarges, the ovarian capsule is increasingly stretched, until it becomes so thin that it breaks. The follicle thus ruptures, and the liquor folliculi, the discus proligerus and the ovum are cast out into the peritoneal cavity. This process is known as ovulation.

At the time of ovulation the fimbrial end of the Fallopian tube lies in close apposition to the ovary so that the fimbriae are ready to catch the ovum when the follicle ruptures (Fig. 4/3). Peritoneal currents also tend to waft the ovum into the tube and once there the ciliated cells of the lumen of the tube together with rhythmic contractions of its muscle wall move the ovum along the tube towards the uterus.

Ovulation is sometimes accompanied by pelvic pain, which is known as Mittelschmerz. This may be due either to the stretching of

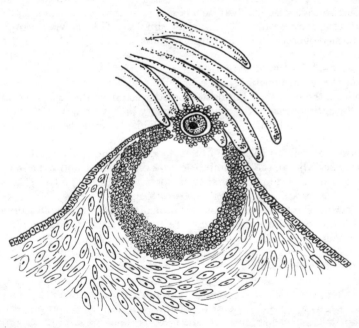

**Fig. 4/3:**   The process of ovulation

the ovarian capsule or to slight bleeding into the peritoneal cavity or to peristalsis in the Fallopian tube occurring at this time.

## The Corpus Luteum

After ovulation has occurred the empty follicle collapses and the lining cells absorb fluid becoming bloated in appearance—a process known as luteinisation. This change affects the cells of both the granulosa layer (granulosa lutein cells) and the theca interna (theca lutein cells). The cells also proliferate and the size of the follicle enlarges so that a solid body, the corpus luteum, is now formed, about 1 to 2cm in diameter, greyish-yellow in appearance and crenated or wavy in outline because of the crumpling of the collapsed walls of the follicle.

Two to three days after ovulation blood vessels develop in the corpus luteum and bleeding may occur into the cavity giving the older corpus luteum a reddish colour and is sometimes known as the corpus haemorrhagicum.

The corpus luteum is developed in five days and is at maximum activity (see later) during the following three to four days. Thereafter it begins to degenerate, the cells becoming vacuolated and the entire structure hyalinised. When degeneration is complete a white structureless body results—the corpus albicans. This is very slowly absorbed over the following 6 to 12 months.

## Hormonal Control of Ovulation

The growth and ripening of the Graafian follicles are under hormonal control, the regulating hormone being derived from the basophil cells of the anterior lobe of the pituitary gland, which is situated within the skull on the under surface of the brain. This hormone belongs to the class of pituitary gonadotrophins, and is known as follicle-stimulating hormone (FSH). It is carried in the bloodstream from the pituitary to the ovary where it causes a follicle to grow and enlarge, and at the same time stimulates the cells of the membrana granulosa and the theca interna to produce hormones called oestrogens.

As the oestrogen levels rise the production of FSH is inhibited until even higher levels of oestrogen are produced which trigger off a surge in the production of a second important pituitary hormone, luteinising hormone (LH). There is a slight but lesser rise in FSH again at the same time and it is at this point that ovulation occurs followed by the formation of the corpus luteum. This produces oestrogens and another hormone called progesterone. In the absence of a pregnancy the corpus luteum degenerates, the levels of oestrogen and progesterone fall, menstruation occurs and the cycle begins again.

It is now realised that the pituitary gland is closely linked to, and influenced by, the hypothalamus which is an adjacent area of the brain. A portal system of veins connects the hypothalamus with the anterior pituitary and via this route substances known as releasing factors are carried from the hypothalamus to the anterior pituitary. These are known collectively as gonadotrophic releasing hormones (GnRH) or, separately, as follicle-stimulating hormone releasing hormone (FSH-RH) and luteinising hormone releasing hormone (LH-RH).

The hypothalamus is connected with the higher centres of the brain and therefore emotional factors can affect its activity and thereby the ovarian and menstrual cycles.

## Hormonal Secretion by the Ovary

It will be seen from the preceding section that the ovary is not only under the hormonal influence of the anterior pituitary gland but it also secretes hormones on its own account.

The main hormone produced by the cells of the membrana granulosa and the theca interna during the development of the Graafian follicle is oestradiol. Oestrone is also produced but is less active. After ovulation oestradiol is secreted in lesser amounts by the corpus luteum and is also formed in the cortex of the suprarenal glands. Oestradiol and oestrone are metabolised in the liver and excreted mainly in the urine as metabolites, at least 20 of which have been identified but the most important of which is oestriol. These substances are known as oestrogens, and are responsible for the secondary sex characteristics which appear in the young girl at the time of puberty, and for some of the changes that occur during the menstrual cycle and pregnancy.

The chief effects induced by oestrogens are:

1. The production of the typical feminine shape of the waist and hips, with soft skin and smooth gentle curves, resulting from the deposition of fat in the subcutaneous tissues which occurs at puberty.

2. The growth of the breasts and nipples, the former being chiefly due to the development of the duct system.

3. The development of the adult vulva and vagina. The squamous epithelium of the vagina, which is thin in childhood, becomes thicker and the superficial cells become cornified after puberty. These cells, when they desquamate, encourage the proliferation of Döderlein's bacilli by virtue of the glycogen they contain, and the increased lactic acid they produce brings about the marked acidity of the adult vagina.

4. The growth of the uterus at puberty, the development of the uterine muscle, and proliferative changes in the endometrium during the menstrual cycle, as described below. The cervical glands also increase in size and produce a greater quantity of mucus, which on

drying crystallises into a pattern resembling fern leaves when seen under a microscope. This result of oestrogenic stimulus constitutes what is known as the 'fern test'.

5. By controlling the releasing factors of the hypothalamus the inhibition of FSH and prolactin from the anterior pituitary and the stimulation of LH. The changes in the levels of FSH and LH are responsible for ovulation, as previously described.

6. The retention of water and electrolytes in the body tissues.

7. Increased coagulability of the blood.

8. During pregnancy, the growth of the uterine muscle, and the ducts of the breasts. It is the continuous high level of oestrogens during this time which, by means of pituitary inhibition suppresses ovulation and lactation in pregnancy.

The cells of the corpus luteum produce another hormone known as progesterone, and a small quantity of oestrogens. The changes produced in the body by progesterone are very important, but they are chiefly manifested during pregnancy, when it is produced in large quantities. Apart from pregnancy its chief function is to produce endometrial changes as part of the menstrual cycle.

The main effects of progesterone are:

1. The production of secretory changes in the endometrium prior to menstruation.

2. To cause slight tingling in the breasts before the onset of menstruation.

3. To cause a slight rise in the body temperature of about half a degree.

4. During pregnancy the effects are:
   (a) The formation of the decidua in the uterus, which enables the fertilised ovum to become embedded.
   (b) The relaxation of the tone of smooth muscle throughout the body.
   (c) The enlargement of the breasts, by growth of the milk-forming alveoli.
   (d) The retention of water and electrolytes in the body tissues in association with oestrogens.

## UTERINE CHANGES ASSOCIATED WITH MENSTRUATION

The uterine changes which relate to menstruation occur in the endometrium as a result of its stimulation by the ovarian hormones, the oestrogens and progesterone. These take the form of the proliferative phase when the endometrium is under the influence of oestrogens, the secretory phase when it is mainly under the influence of oestrogens and progesterone together, and finally the actual phase of menstruation itself.

## The Proliferative Phase

This begins at the end of a menstrual period, when the actual loss of menstrual blood ceases, and lasts thereafter for about 10 days. During this time a Graafian follicle is ripening in an ovary, and it is the oestrogens from the granulosa cells and theca interna of the follicle which are responsible for the changes which take place.

These consist of the repair of the denuded endometrium, whose superficial layer has been cast off during menstruation, by growth from the unchanged deeper layer, and its subsequent hypertrophy until it is 2 to 3mm thick.

The structure of this proliferated endometrium is as follows (Fig. 4/4):

1. A basal layer about 1mm in thickness, which lies on the myometrium. It consists of a loose connective tissue containing spindle cells, lymphocytes collected into lymphatic nodes, and blood vessels.

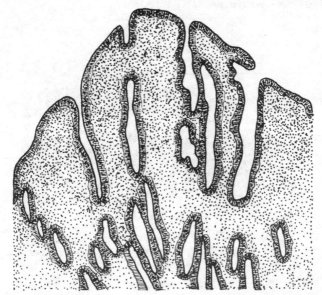

**Fig. 4/4:** Diagrammatic representation of low power magnification of proliferative endometrium, showing the straight tubular glands under the influence of oestrogen

It contains the tips or extremities of the tubular uterine glands, some of which terminate in this layer, while others invade the myometrium for a short distance. This zone remains unchanged during all the phases of menstruation.

2. A superficial layer, 2.5mm in thickness, composed of loose connective tissue containing tubular glands, spindle cells, blood vessels and lymphatics. This is known as the functional layer. The tubular glands are narrow, of uniform width, and pass straight from the surface down to the basal layer.

3. The epithelium which covers the functional layer is cuboidal and ciliated in places. It is this epithelium which dips down into the endometrium to form the tubular glands.

## The Secretory Phase
After the proliferative phase of the endometrium has been in existence for about 10 days, ovulation occurs in the ovary and the corpus luteum is formed. The progesterone from the corpus luteum produces the following changes in the endometrium, which constitute the secretory phase which lasts for 14 days (Fig. 4/5):

1. The basal layer remains unchanged.

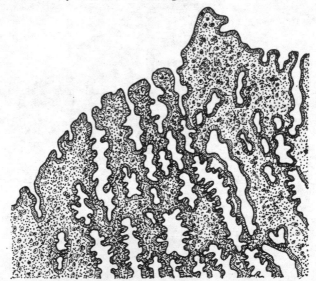

**Fig. 4/5:**   Diagrammatic representation of low power magnification of secretory endometrium, showing corkscrew glands under the influence of progesterone

2. The functional layer increases in thickness up to 3.5mm. The glands become widened and dilated, and further increase in length so that they become corkscrew-shaped; their cells are filled with secretion which passes into the lumen of the glands. The spindle cells become enlarged and are clumped together mainly in the superficial zone of the endometrium. The functional layer after the twenty-first day of the cycle comes to consist of two zones, (a) a superficial compact zone filled with swollen stromal cells and (b) a deeper spongy layer composed of dilated glands lying in a loose connective tissue framework. Towards the end of the 14 days the endometrium becomes increasingly vascular and congested.

3. The surface epithelium remains unchanged.

### The Menstrual Phase

After 14 days of life the corpus luteum degenerates, the supply of oestrogens and progesterone is cut off from the endometrium and in consequence the functional layer dies. It is the disintegration of the functional layer of the endometrium, with consequent bleeding, which constitutes the actual menstrual flow. The arteries in the endometrium are spiral in form; immediately before menstruation begins, short segments of these vessels go into intermittent spasm. At the same time anastomotic channels open up between the arterioles and veins in the superficial layers of the endometrium, so that the blood is shunted from the arterioles directly into the veins, and the circulation through the capillaries of the superficial layers is brought to a standstill. Deprived of its circulation, the functional part of the endometrium undergoes necrosis and sloughs off, being subsequently expelled from the uterus by muscular contractions. It is this tissue, accompanied by bleeding from disrupted blood vessels, which actually forms the menstrual flow. This usually continues for about five days, the total amount of blood lost amounting to an average of 50ml. The presence of fibrinolysins prevents the blood from clotting unless excessive bleeding occurs when clots will be passed in the menstrual flow. The ovum in a degenerated state is also passed during this time.

At the end of this phase a new endometrium is reconstituted from the unchanged basal layer containing the terminal deep portions of the tubular glands, as already described.

## RELATION OF MENSTRUATION TO OVULATION

It will be understood that normal menstruation is completely dependent upon the hormonal changes associated with ovulation, which are themselves related to changes in the anterior lobe of the pituitary gland. Ovulation occurs 14 days before the onset of the next menstrual period, and as the ovum only remains capable of being fertilised for 24 to 48 hours thereafter, women are thus in their most fertile state about 14 days before the next menstrual period is expected.

The menstrual rhythm may be tabulated thus:

|   |   | Duration in Days |
|---|---|---|
| 1. | Following menstruation there is growth of a follicle; production of oestrogens; proliferative changes in the endometrium | 10 |
| 2. | Ovulation | — |
| 3. | Growth of a corpus luteum; progesterone production with a small amount of oestrogens; secretory changes in the endometrium | 14 |
| 4. | Degeneration of corpus luteum and menstruation | 4 |
|   | Total | 28 |

This sequence occurs every four weeks under normal circumstances, and in the absence of pregnancy, from the time of puberty until the menopause. Individual variations in these figures are, however, quite common. Thus menstruation may last from two to seven days, and may occur at intervals of three to six weeks and still be quite normal. Ovulation, however, in these cases, always occurs about 14 days before the onset of the next period, so that the length of the secretory phase is approximately constant, while the proliferative phase varies with the duration of the cycle.

## Significance of Menstruation

The whole of the menstrual process is a preparation for pregnancy because the fertilised ovum needs a rich and vascular bed in which to implant and develop. The secretory endometrium, formed after ovulation, provides such a suitable nidus for the development of the fertilised ovum. If such an ovum is not produced the endometrium is cast off after 14 days and a new one begins to grow. It is important to understand the menstrual cycle in terms of the close association of the hypothalamic/pituitary and ovarian functions. A summary of events may help understanding.

1. Hypothalamic GnRH stimulates the anterior pituitary to release FSH and LH into the circulation. Initially, mainly FSH is released with only small amounts of LH.

2. FSH stimulates a few sensitive follicles in the ovary to mature and oestrogen is produced from their surrounding theca cells.

3. The rising concentration of oestrogen feeds back to the hypothalamus and the pituitary in a negative way reducing the amount of FSH produced by the pituitary.

4. Oestrogen levels continue to rise and reach a peak (Fig. 4/6). This produces a positive feedback with a sudden surge of LH which induces ovulation within the next 16 to 24 hours. A small surge of FSH occurs but it is the LH surge which is essential for ovulation.

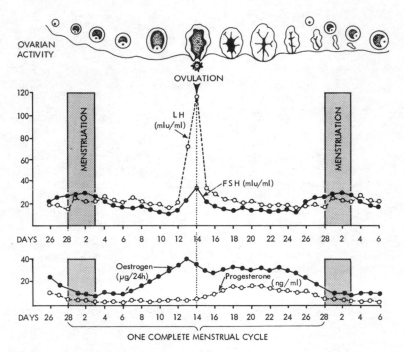

**Fig. 4/6:** The menstrual cycle showing the relation of ovarian and endometrial changes

5. One follicle outstrips the others, releases its ovum and then collapses. The corpus luteum so formed produces progesterone.

6. The circulating progesterone added to the circulating oestrogen exerts a negative feedback effect on the hypothalamus and pituitary and FSH and LH levels fall.

7. Unless fertilisation and implantation of the ovum occur the corpus luteum degenerates, oestrogen and progesterone secretion falls, and becomes insufficient to support the endometrium. If this is the case,

approximately 14 days after ovulation, the endometrium breaks down, its blood vessels rupture and bleeding, viz. menstruation, occurs.

8. With degeneration of the corpus luteum the negative feedback mechanism fails and this allows the hypothalamus to produce GnRH again. A new cycle has been initiated.

# Chapter Five

# The Cell:
# Development of the Ovum

## THE CELL

All living plants and animals (including man) have a structure composed essentially of cells and cellular products. The cells which form the human body number many thousands of millions and although their size usually lies between $10\mu$ and $100\mu$, their individual shape and dimensions differ according to the organ or tissue in which they occur. Thus liver cells, kidney cells, brain cells, etc., have different characteristics dependent on their varying functions and yet they all have basically the same constituents.

Each cell, when it is in its resting stage and is not dividing, consists of a semi-fluid jelly-like material known as protoplasm, which is bounded by a delicate cell membrane. Immersed in it and usually central in position lies a small globule of denser material that stains readily with certain dyes and is known as the nucleus of the cell. The protoplasm that surrounds it is called the cytoplasm.

### The cell membrane
This is a fine pellicle that encloses the cell and acts as a retaining and protective membrane, and at the same time regulates the passage of fluid and dissolved substances in and out of the cell.

### The nucleus
Under the microscope this appears to be a uniform collection of dense stainable material, known as chromatin, but in reality it is composed of separate masses of chromatin immersed in a fluid called nuclear sap or karyoplasm, and enclosed by a fine nuclear membrane. It is this material that forms the chromosomes during cell division. In places there may occur small more darkly staining condensations of chromatin, which are known as nucleoli. The properties and behaviour of the nucleus during cell division are described below.

## The cytoplasm

This is composed of water in which are present proteins, fats or lipids, carbohydrates, secretory granules, vacuoles, and dissolved inorganic and organic salts, particularly potassium salts. Also present are certain particles visible under the microscope which are sometimes called the organelles:

1. A single (sometimes double) small body known as a centriole, which is surrounded by a zone of clear cytoplasm to form a centrosome. This lies close to the nucleus and plays a part in the process of cell division.

2. Multiple small structures known as mitochondria. These are minute rod like bodies scattered throughout the cytoplasm which produce energy by a process whereby a substance they contain known as adenosine triphosphate (ATP) changes to adenosine diphosphate (ADP) with the release of energy. It is this energy that enables the cell to carry out its function, e.g. the muscle cell to contract, the glandular cell to secrete or the nerve cell to transmit an electrical impulse.

3. The Golgi apparatus is a collection of minute rods and granules which form a reticular pattern. Its exact significance is not properly understood, but it is believed to modify cellular secretions.

4. The endoplasmic reticulum is a diffuse network of membranous structure scattered throughout the cytoplasm and only visible under very great magnification. It plays a part in the synthesis of proteins within the cell.

## THE PROCESS OF CELL DIVISION

There are two types of cell division that have to be studied. First, the division that occurs during the normal process of cell growth when a single cell divides into two identical daughter cells—this is known as mitosis. Second, a special form of division occurs in both sexes when the reproductive cells are formed—this is called meiosis.

### Mitosis

The process of mitosis by which a cell divides and gives rise to two daughter cells begins with changes in the centrosome and nucleus which lead to splitting of the nucleus into two nuclei, followed by changes in the cytoplasm and cell membrane which result in the production of two new cells. The nuclear changes are described as occurring in four phases (Fig. 5/1):

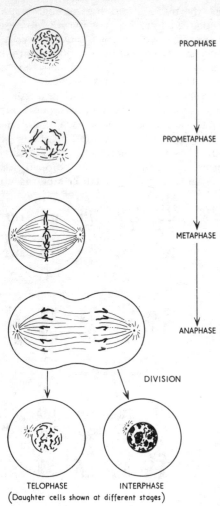

**Fig. 5/1:** Stages of mitosis

*Prophase*

The centriole, if single, splits into two centrioles which separate from
each other but remain connected by a star-shaped pattern of radiating
filaments in the cytoplasm (Fig. 5/1). At the same time the appearance
of the chromatin in the nucleus alters and it becomes revealed as a
conglomerate of individual fine threads or filaments known as

chromosomes; the nucleoli and nuclear membrane disappear and become incorporated into the pattern of chromosomes. As these changes take place the two centrioles move into position one on each side of the nucleus at opposite poles, and the former star-pattern of fibrils becomes a spindle that extends between them and passes through the cluster of chromosomes.

When the chromosomes are examined under high powers of magnification, each is seen to be composed of two filaments adherent along their lengths and coiled around each other. These are known as chromatids. Each species of animal and plant has its own individual number of chromosomes which is always constant under normal conditions of growth. This is called the diploid number and in the human race is 46 (Fig. 5/2). Of this number 44 chromosomes are

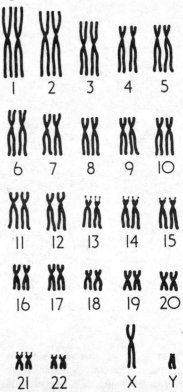

**Fig. 5/2:** Human chromosomes arranged as 22 homologous pairs of auto-somes and the X and Y sex chromosomes

concerned with growth and development and are called autosomes, while two are concerned with sex and are known as the sex chromosomes. Half of the chromosomes have been derived from the original ovum which has given rise to the cell and are thus maternal in origin, and half have come from the original fertilising spermatozoon and so are paternal in origin.

At one place in each chromosome the chromatids are fused—this point is known as the centromere.

It can also be seen that the autosomes occur in pairs, i.e., although they are of different shapes and sizes with the centromere placed in different positions along their length, each one has an identical fellow with which it becomes paired—these are homologous chromosomes, one of the pair being maternal and the other paternal in origin. Thus in man there are 22 pairs of homologous chromosomes and two sex chromosomes (Fig. 5/2).

Each individual chromosome is composed of a substance called deoxyribonucleic acid (DNA), which is not evenly distributed along the length of the chromosome but occurs in localised nodules, like beads on a string. These are the genes and there are about 2000 of them present in each autosome. They are responsible for handing on to the daughter cells the qualities and properties of the mother cell. They are thus the locus of heredity.

*Metaphase*
The chromosomes become attached in a circle around the equator of the spindle that extends between the two centrioles (Fig. 5/1).

*Anaphase*
The centromere of each chromosome splits into two halves and this is followed by the separation of the chromatids along their entire length. Each original chromosome therefore divides longitudinally into two new chromosomes which are identical in structure to each other and to their parent chromosome (Fig. 5/1). These new chromosomes appear to repel each other, and travel in opposite directions along the threads of the spindle towards the two centrioles. As they approach these bodies they become grouped together, there being the same number of chromosomes in each group as there were chromosomes in the original cell, half still being maternal and the other half paternal in origin.

*Telophase*
A nuclear membrane forms around each group of daughter chromosomes as they gradually lose their individuality and merge together to

form a new nucleus of each daughter cell (Fig. 5/1). As this forms new nucleoli make their appearance.

Following this splitting of the nucleus, the cell membrane becomes indented around the cell in the plane of cleavage, and the cytoplasm gradually becomes divided into two halves, each of which surrounds one of the new nuclei. The cell membrane then encloses each division of the cytoplasm so that two new daughter cells, each with its nucleus, centrosome, cytoplasm and organelles, and cell membrane have been formed from the original cell. At first each daughter cell is smaller than the original cell, but in the process of normal growth it enlarges so that in due course it becomes identical with its predecessor.

The whole process of mitosis takes about one hour to occur.

## Meiosis
This type of cell division occurs in the formation of the reproductive cells or gametes, i.e., the ovum in the female and the spermatozoon in the male. This involves a double type of cleavage:

### First Cleavage

### Prophase
This is similar to the mitotic prophase in that a spindle develops in the usual way between the two centrioles and the chromosomes in homologous pairs become demarcated. However, as each chromosome separates into its two constituent chromatids the homologous chromosomes become coiled closely around each other and chromatin becomes exchanged between them. In this way there is an interchange of genetic material between chromosomes derived from maternal and paternal sources. After this exchange the chromosomes uncoil and separate.

### Metaphase
The 23 pairs of chromosomes become attached to the equator of the spindle as in mitosis.

### Anaphase
The important distinction from mitosis now occurs. The chromosomes do not divide longitudinally but instead each member of an homologous pair becomes drawn along the spindle away from its partner towards one of the two centrioles, so that each daughter nucleus as it is formed contains only 23 chromosomes, i.e., one chromosome of each original pair. This is sometimes called the reduction division.

## Telophase

The formation of two new nuclei with their nuclear membranes takes place and this is followed by the division of the cytoplasm and cell membrane.

This new number of chromosomes in the daughter cells (23) is said to be the haploid number in distinction to the original diploid number of 46.

## Second Cleavage

### Prophase

Immediately after the preceding telophase, the nuclear membrane disappears and the changes of prophase are seen again with the formation of the centrioles and spindle.

### Metaphase

The 23 chromosomes become attached to the spindle in the usual way.

### Anaphase

Each chromosome splits longitudinally as in mitosis, and the separated chromatids pass to opposite poles.

### Telophase

This occurs normally, the new nuclei and nuclear membranes being formed in the usual way.

The results of these changes are that four cells have formed from the original cell, the first cleavage producing two cells with the haploid number of chromosomes as a result of the reduction division, and the second cleavage increasing these to four cells. Not only are the chromosomes of these cells half the original number but they also have a different genetic content as a result of the chromatin interchange.

In the human female this process is intimately associated with ovulation and fertilisation. In the primordial follicles of the newborn baby the ova, which may be called primary oocytes, have begun the first cleavage of meiosis, but the process goes no further and the nucleus of the cell remains in the prophase state during childhood and does not proceed to metaphase and anaphase. This arrested state is known as the dictyate stage. Immediately preceding ovulation, under the influence of luteinising hormone, the first cleavage is finally completed, resulting in the halving of the number of chromosomes as described above, one half being cast off as the first polar body and the other half remaining in the ovum, which may now be termed the secondary oocyte. The second cleavage, resulting in the expulsion of the second polar body, only takes place if fertilisation occurs.

In the human male spermatozoa are formed from large cells known as spermatogonia in the testicle. These divide into primary spermatocytes containing 46 chromosomes, each of which undergoes meiotic or reduction division into two secondary spermatocytes, containing 23 chromosomes, and then into four spermatids, without the production of any polar bodies. Each spermatid then grows and develops into a spermatozoon with a complement therefore of 23 chromosomes.

It will thus be seen that immediately prior to fertilisation, the ovum and the spermatozoon each contains 23 chromosomes.


**Fertilisation**

Following the entry of the spermatozoon into the ovum, the head and neck becomes detached from the middle piece and tail which disappear and are no longer recognisable in the cytoplasm of the ovum. The head of the sperm swells and becomes the male pronucleus, while changes of prophase produce the 23 chromosomes. At the same time the nucleus of the ovum completes its second cleavage as already described and becomes the female pronucleus, the second polar body being extruded into the perivitelline space.

Approximation and fusion of the two pronuclei next occur. A centrosome believed to contain the centriole from the sperm, divides and forms the characteristic spindle. The two sets of 23 chromosomes from the two pronuclei arrange themselves around the equator of the spindle as in metaphase in such a way that the corresponding homologous chromosomes lie alongside each other, one coming from the ovum and one from the sperm. The fertilised ovum or zygote now contains the diploid number of 46 chromosomes.

The chromosomes then split in anaphase and are drawn along the spindle to opposite poles in telophase and two daughter cells are produced in the manner already described. This is the first step in segmentation of the zygote.


## THE CHEMICAL STRUCTURE OF CHROMOSOMES

It has already been stated that chromosomes are composed of chromatin, arranged as a succession of genes to form a filament or thread. The chief chemical constituent of chromatin and the genes is a nucleoprotein which contains a type of nucleic acid known as deoxyribonucleic acid (DNA). The cytoplasm of the cell contains a similar substance known as ribonucleic acid (RNA). These are both of outstanding importance to the life and functions of the cell.

DNA has a high molecular weight and the atoms of which the molecules are composed form long chains which wind around each other like a spiral or helix, being connected along their length by transverse bonds. The structure of the molecule is thus like a ladder which is twisted on itself.

The chains winding around each other (corresponding to the sides of the ladder) consist of many sugar (deoxyribose) and phosphate groups joined together, while the transverse bonds (corresponding to the rungs) linking them together are composed of four bases joined up in pairs. These bases are adenine, thymine, guanine and cytosine occurring in regular sequence. A unit consisting of a base, sugar and phosphate group is known as a nucleotide, millions of which make up a single chromosome.

The genes manufacture the second form of nucleic acid, RNA, which contains a different sugar (ribose) and an alternative base (uracil). This enters the cytoplasm and there forms proteins and enzymes which are typical of the cell, and thereby confer upon it its qualities and enable it to carry out its functions.

As a result of the double structure of the DNA molecule, it is able to split along its entire length, after which each half can duplicate itself and reform the complete molecule. In this way DNA is able to reproduce and perpetuate itself.

During the process of cell growth and division this property of perpetuation enables the DNA to remain constant during the lifetime of the cell and its descendants. When mitosis occurs the mother cell thus hands on identical genes to each of the daughter cells; during meiosis the qualities of the parent cell inherent in its genes are passed to the reproductive cell, and ultimately to the new individual.

The sequence of nucleotides along the length of the DNA molecular chains varies, and this variation, occurring in different genes, endows each gene with its individual properties. These differences influence the RNA manufactured, and this in its turn produces different proteins and enzymes and so gives rise to the different cells of the body. These differing genes of the chromosomes constitute the genotype of the individual, while his resultant physical characteristics comprise his phenotype.

It can be understood that the genes of the chromosomes, through the medium of RNA and the cell proteins and enzymes, control the functions of the cell. When it is remembered that this is occurring in all the millions of cells of the body, and that the genes which control it are derived equally from maternal and paternal sources, the nature of heredity can be appreciated.

## SEX CHROMOSOMES

The role of sex chromosomes in determining sex is described on p. 115, but they have additional features of interest. Cells of the female body (apart from the reproductive cells) contain 44 autosomes and two X sex chromosomes. These two X sex chromosomes have been derived from different sources—one has come from the maternal ovum and one from the paternal spermatozoon. Only one of these X chromosomes appears to participate in the normal functioning of the cell, and so disappears within the chromatin mass of the nucleus when the cell is in the resting phase. The other X chromosome remains unchanged and can be seen under favourable circumstances as a black-staining body about one micron in diameter within the nuclear membrane. It can most easily be identified in certain types of cell such as the squamous cells lining the buccal cavity, when it is referred to as a Barr body or sex chromatin (Fig. 5/3). Sometimes, such as in polymorphonuclear leucocytes in the circulating blood, it appears to project through the nuclear membrane into the cytoplasm, when it is termed a 'drum-stick' (Fig. 5/4). Examination of these cells from normal individuals, there-fore, will reveal the sex to which they belong. If the Barr body or drumstick is present the cell contains two X chromosomes and is said to be chromatin positive, and comes from a female; if there is no Barr body or drumstick in any of the cells visualised then the cell contains only one X chromosome and is said to be chromatin negative, and so comes from a male.

This procedure is of use in determining the true sex in a case of intersex or hermaphroditism, and is sometimes employed during pregnancy, when the liquor amnii may be tapped and the nuclei of fetal or amniotic cells contained in it will reveal the sex of the fetus.

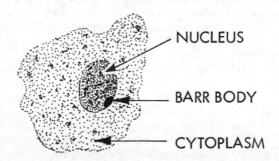

**Fig. 5/3:**   A cell showing a Barr body

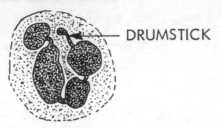

Fig. 5/4:    A leucocyte showing a 'drumstick'

It has been suggested that of the two X chromosomes in each female cell one has genes that are active and participate in the function of the cell, while the other forming the Barr body has inactive genes. Each of these chromosomes may be derived from either maternal or paternal sources—it follows therefore that some cells will have a functioning maternal X chromosome while others will have a functioning paternal X chromosome. These cells then may be expected to give rise to different behaviour patterns dependent upon the different origin of their X chromosome. Such differences account for the colour patchiness in the coats of mice and tortoiseshell cats, and also for the absence of a specific enzyme from the red cells of women.

**Abnormal Separation of Chromosomes**
The process of meiosis involved in the formation of the reproductive cells does not invariably occur in a normal manner. Departure from the normal may occur in many ways, but only those most frequently encountered will now be described. Altogether, with the possible exception of mongolism or Down's syndrome, they are rare. They mostly arise during anaphase, when the chromosomes are splitting and the two halves are being drawn apart towards the centrioles. They occur most frequently in parents towards the end of their reproductive life, when the process of meiosis has lost its vigour and efficiency.

*Down's syndrome*
In this condition the separation of one homologous chromosome pair (number 21) does not occur, with the result that two chromosomes instead of one of a pair are drawn towards one centriole, and none goes towards the other. The result is that one daughter cell has one chromosome too many (that is 24) and the other has one too few (22). The second cell does not survive, but should the former be involved in fertilisation then the new individual will have 47 chromosomes in each cell, 24 being derived from the abnormal cell and 23 from the other fertilising cell. This non-separation of the chromosomes is known as

non-disjunction. The individual with 47 chromosomes develops into a patient with Down's syndrome or mongolism and is said to have trisomy-21. It will be noticed that the sex chromosomes are not involved in this malfunction, so that the syndrome may occur in persons of each sex.

### Turner's syndrome

In this abnormality the sex chromosomes are affected. Non-disjunction of the two X chromosomes in the ovum similarly occurs so that there are some ova with no X chromosomes and some with two X chromosomes. If fertilisation occurs between any X-bearing sperm and the former cell, the new individual will have only 45 chromosomes in each cell of type XO, because one X chromosome from the ovum is missing. This can also result from non-disjunction in the formation of spermatozoa, when a sperm carrying no sex chromosome fertilises a normal ovum containing a single X chromosome. Such a person has cells that are chromatin negative and is said to be an example of Turner's syndrome or gonadal dysgenesis. The incidence of this condition is about 1 in 2 500 persons.

Such an individual grows up outwardly resembling a female although she has infantile sex organs, inactive 'streak' ovaries, is very short with scanty hirsutes, has a wide 'webbed' neck, a wide carrying angle of the arms (cubitus valgus), and deformities of the ears and digits. These persons always have amenorrhoea and are always sterile.

### Superfemale

These cases also result from non-disjunction (Fig. 5/5), but in this event an ovum containing two X chromosomes as described above is fertilised by an X-bearing spermatozoon, and the resultant individual has three X sex chromosomes and a total complement of 47 chromosomes to the cell. Two Barr bodies are present in these cases. However, in distinction from what the name suggests, these persons usually grow up with an infantile genital tract, oligomenorrhoea and sterility, and perhaps mental deficiency. The incidence is about 1 in 1 000.

### Klinefelter's syndrome

Another result of non-disjunction may be that a two X-bearing ovum unites with a Y-bearing sperm to produce an individual with three sex chromosomes, XXY, and a total of 47. This state of affairs might also result from a normal X-bearing ovum uniting with an XY-bearing sperm. The result is to produce a person who resembles a male (because his cells contain a Y chromosome), but who is chromatin positive (because like a female he has two X chromosomes). Such a

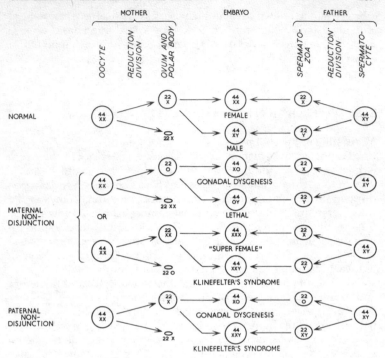

**Fig. 5/5:**    Examples of non-disjunction

person is said to be an example of Klinefelter's syndrome (Fig. 5/5). He is usually tall with infantile testicles, large breasts, and perhaps mental defects, and although he is able to have sexual intercourse he will be sterile. The incidence is about 1 in 500.

*Mosaicism*
Abnormalities of development may not occur in such clear-cut clinical entities as the above. Sometimes individuals are seen particularly in cases of intersex, where some abnormal features are present but not all. For example, some individuals show an intermediate state between Turner's syndrome and a normal female, or between the syndrome and a normal male. These persons are likely to have some cells with an XO chromosome pattern and some with the normal XX female pattern or the normal XY male pattern. Such cases probably result from non-disjunction of sex chromosomes occurring early in the development of the embryo after fertilisation; the resultant differing

cells are handed down to their successors so that some tissues of the individual have a different chromosome constitution from others. There are numerous types of this phenomenon, and such individuals are said to be mosaics.

## THE DEVELOPMENT OF THE FERTILISED OVUM

### Maturation of the Ovum

Prior to the act of ovulation, certain changes take place in the ovum (while it is still within the Graafian follicle) which constitute what is known as the maturation of the ovum. This consists essentially of a division of the ovum, whereby the number of chromosomes in the nucleus is reduced from 46, the normal number in human beings, to 23.

Normally when every cell in the body divides, the nucleus splits up into 46 small threads of nuclear material known as chromosomes. These become divided longitudinally during normal cell division so that each daughter cell still contains the full number of 46 chromosomes. Exceptions to this rule occur during maturation of the ovum and during development of the spermatozoa from the primary spermatocytes in the male testes, when the number of chromosomes is halved, so that the human reproductive cells each contain only 23.

Each chromosome is composed of clumps of nuclear material, in the same way that a chain is made up of links. These are known as genes and it is these genes which impart to the individual his specific physical, mental and moral characteristics which together make up his appearance, intellectual powers and behaviour.

When maturation of the ovum takes place the two resultant cells, each containing 23 chromosomes, are very unequal in size. One cell is still called the ovum and exactly resembles the ovum in size before maturation; the second cell is very small and consists merely of nuclear material surrounded by a small amount of cytoplasm. This cell is known as the first polar body. It may be said, then, that the ovum undergoes maturation prior to ovulation by casting off the first polar body.

### Fertilisation of the Ovum

After ovulation the ovum surrounded by its mantle of cells, the corona radiata (Fig. 5/6), is received into the Fallopian tube. It passes slowly down the tube towards the uterus, moving along as a result of waves of peristalsis in the walls of the tube, aided by currents set up by the ciliary action of the lining cells. During this time the ovum receives

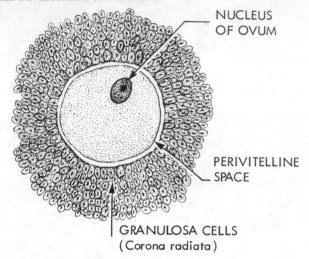

NUCLEUS
OF OVUM

PERIVITELLINE
SPACE

GRANULOSA CELLS
(Corona radiata)

**Fig. 5/6:**  An ovum surrounded by the discus proligerus

food partly from the cells of the corona, and partly from secretions of
the cells in the mucosa of the Fallopian tube.

When sexual intercourse occurs semen containing a large number of
spermatozoa is deposited in the upper vagina. The liberality of natural
processes is again here demonstrated, because the actual number of
spermatozoa ejaculated at this time is about 300 000 000 of which only
one is necessary to effect fertilisation.

The human spermatozoon is a small structure 52 to 62$\mu$ in length,
shaped rather like a tadpole, and comprising a head, neck, middle
piece and tail (Fig. 5/7). The head, which is the nucleus, is shaped like a
pointed oval, and is covered by a hemispherical cap known as the
head-cap or acrosome. It contains 23 chromosomes and is largely
composed of DNA. Next to the head is a small constricted neck which
contains the centriole of the cell. The middle piece consists of an axial
bundle of fibrils surrounded by a coiled sheath of mitochondria, the
fibrils being continued down the long tail. It is by lashing movements
of the tail that the spermatozoon is able to travel along the female
genital tract, covering its own length in three seconds, a speed corresponding to 7.5cm an hour. These movements of the tail are controlled by the mitochondria, which use a special form of sugar known
as fructose in the semen as a source of energy.

After the act of intercourse many of the spermatozoa are killed by
the lactic acid present in the vaginal fluid. Spermatozoa live best in an

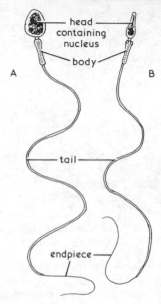

**Fig. 5/7:**   Spermatozoa.   A. Showing component parts
                             B. The side view

alkaline medium, and this is provided by the secretion of alkaline
mucus from the cervical glands. Thus after a few hours many of the
spermatozoa are killed, but those that have reached the haven of a
drop of cervical mucus survive; they are then able to reach the external os, to work their way up the cervical canal, and to pass through
the uterine cavity into the Fallopian tubes.

The spermatozoa which enter the tubes are able to travel against the
direction of peristalsis and ciliary flow by virtue of the propelling
action of their tails. Those which have entered the tube containing the
ovum reach it in the outer third of the Fallopian tube. The ovum
remains capable of fertilisation for only 24 hours, and possibly only for
8–12 hours, after ovulation, during which time it occupies this part of
the tube.

Many spermatozoa arrive at the discus proligerus which they then
have to penetrate in order to reach the ovum. They are able to do this
by means of an enzyme which they carry known as hyaluronidase.
This breaks down the cementing substance holding the cells of the
discus together without actually destroying them—the spermatozoa
are thus able to pass between the cells to reach the ovum. One

spermatozoon then unites with it by entering into its substance. As soon as this occurs the cell membrane becomes impenetrable and no further spermatozoa are able to effect a union. This entry of a spermatozoon into the ovum constitutes the essential feature of fertilisation.

After the entry the head of the spermatozoon forms a mass of nuclear material, containing 23 chromosomes (Fig. 5/8), which is known as the male pronucleus; the middle piece and tail drop off and are merged into the cytoplasm of the ovum. The other unwanted spermatozoa throughout the female genital tract atrophy and disappear.

Following the entry of the spermatozoon, further changes take place in the nucleus of the ovum, whereby a second polar body is formed and cast off. There is no further reduction in the number of chromosomes at this division, so that the now mature ovum and the second polar body each contain 23 chromosomes (Fig. 5/9). The first polar body may also divide at this time so that three polar bodies may be present alongside the ovum; these however serve no known function, but degenerate and disappear. The nucleus of the mature ovum is now known as the female pronucleus. The cell thus contains a male pronucleus of 23 chromosomes and a female pronucleus of 23 chromosomes; fusion of these two structures then occurs and a cell containing 46 chromosomes results.

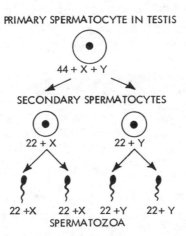

**Fig. 5/8:** Scheme showing development of spermatozoa also containing a reduced number of chromosomes

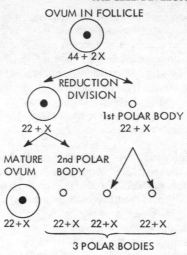

**Fig. 5/9:**  Scheme showing maturation of ovum with reduction in the number
of chromosomes

This cell is a new individual and is known as a zygote (Fig. 5/10). The
qualities it possesses derived from its genes, come half from its mother
and half from its father; although its nutrition is derived solely from its
mother for many months, yet it is a true blend of the qualities of its two
parents.

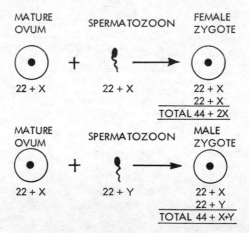

**Fig. 5/10:**  Scheme illustrating the formation of male and female zygotes

   At the time of fusion of the pronuclei the sex of the new individual
is decided. This is because the sex of the individual is a function of
its constituent chromosomes. Thus the human cell of 46 chromosomes is made up of 44 ordinary chromosomes, known as autosomes,
plus two sex chromosomes of different kinds, one known as X and
the other as Y. Female cells contain 44 plus 2 X chromosomes, and
male cells 44 plus X plus Y. After the reduction division all ova contain 22 plus X chromosomes, while spermatozoa are of two kinds
—some contain 22 plus X, while others contain 22 plus Y. The sex of
the zygote depends upon the kind of spermatozoon which effects
fertilisation; if this is done by a 22 plus X type, the zygote will contain
44 plus 2 X chromosomes and will develop into a female; if a 22 plus Y
type, it will contain 44 plus X plus Y, and will consequently become
male. The sex of the offspring, in human beings, is thus solely dependent upon the father.

### Segmentation of the Ovum
At the time of fertilisation the ovum is still within the zona pellucida
and corona radiata lying in the outer third of the Fallopian tube. After
fertilisation the zygote travels along the tube and reaches the uterus in
about four days, being nourished by secretions from the goblet cells in
the epithelium lining the tube and by degenerating cells of the discus
proligerus. During this time the zygote divides into two cells, then into
four and eight, and so on. This process is known as the segmentation
of the fertilised ovum, and the mass of cells produced, about 0.5mm in
diameter, is known as the morula (Fig. 5/11). The zona pellucida serves

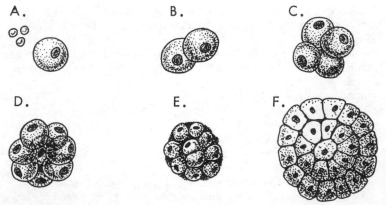

**Fig. 5/11:**   Segmentation of the ovum  (F) = the morula

to bind the cells together and to prevent their adherence to the walls of the tube, but it disappears by the time the cavity of the uterus is reached.

During this journey some fluid appears between the cells of the morula and a small cystic structure 2mm in diameter, known as the blastocyst, is formed (Fig. 5/12). It is at this stage that the fertilised

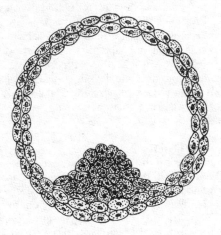

**Fig. 5/12:**  A blastocyst

ovum enters the uterine cavity, four days after fertilisation and five or six days after ovulation. The capsule of the blastocyst is composed of a layer of cells known as the trophoblast, while at one pole is collected a small mass of cells which is called the inner cell mass. As the blastocyst lies in the uterine cavity (Fig. 5/13) the cells of the trophoblast lie adjacent to the surface of the secretory endometrium; from the time of the seventh day after fertilisation two simultaneous events begin to occur, namely the formation of the decidua and the embedding of the ovum.

**The Formation of the Decidua**

As the embedding of the ovum is in progress, changes occur in the secretory endometrium which result in its becoming transformed into the decidua. These changes are as follows:

1. The endometrium hypertrophies, reaching 6 to 8mm in thickness.

2. The stroma becomes increasingly vascular and oedematous.

3. The stroma cells swell and enlarge with the result that they become closely packed together in the superficial part of the functional

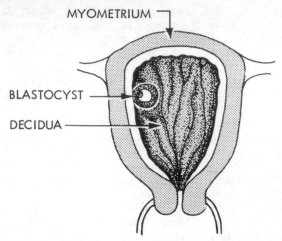

**Fig. 5/13:**    A blastocyst in the uterus before the process of embedding

layer. They now form what is known as the compact layer. These new cells, which are called decidual cells, are polygonal in shape as a result of the mutual pressure they exert upon each other.

4. The tubular glands become more tortuous and dilated in their deeper parts, and their lumina are packed with secretion. This increased dilatation below the compact part of the functional layer produces a spongy cavernous appearance; it is known as the cavernous or spongy layer.

5. The basal layer remains unchanged.

The decidua thus is thicker, more rich and vascular than the secretory endometrium. The division of the functional layer into compact and spongy layers is much more marked, partly owing to the production of the decidual cells, which render the superficial portion of the decidua practically solid, and partly to the enlarged glands which change the deeper portion into a net-like formation. The decidual cells are a characteristic feature of pregnancy, and rarely occur apart from it.

This development of the decidua results from an increased output of progesterone from the corpus luteum. Accordingly it is found that the corpus luteum in the presence of pregnancy does not degenerate in the usual way at the fourteenth day after ovulation, but instead continues to grow and develop. In fact, it increases in size up to the twelfth week of pregnancy, when it becomes cystic and occupies one-third of the entire ovary. It is this greatly enlarged corpus luteum of pregnancy which provides the progesterone responsible for the building up of the decidua; also as degeneration does not occur, there is no death of the endometrium and no menstruation; hence this increased growth of the corpus luteum and production of progesterone are responsible for the amenorrhoea associated with pregnancy.

The stimulus which makes the corpus luteum develop in the presence of an embedding ovum is hormonal. A gonadotrophic hormone is produced from the cells of the trophoblast as they invade the lining of the uterus. This hormone, known as chorionic gonado-trophin, is absorbed into the maternal blood from the invading trophoblast, and is carried to the ovary. Here it augments the action of LH from the anterior pituitary, with the result that increased growth and development of the corpus luteum ensue.

It is this hormone, chorionic gonadotrophin, which, excreted in the maternal urine, is used as a basis for the immunological pregnancy tests which are available.


## THE EMBEDDING OF THE OVUM

As the blastocyst rests on the surface of the endometrium where it is nourished by secretions from the endometrial glands, the trophoblast cells secrete enzymes which digest the endometrial cells and so form a small scooped-out depression in which the blastocyst rests. This begins about the seventh day after fertilisation. The digestive process continues and the blastocyst sinks deeper and deeper into what is now becoming the decidua, the deepest cells constituting the entering pole, to which the inner cell mass is attached. Finally the whole blastocyst is received into the decidua, the last portion to enter being the closing pole, and the superficial part of the decidua closes over the blastocyst, its site of entry being marked by a small fibrin plug (Fig. 5/14).

At this stage the blastocyst forms a small nodule lying in the decidual lining of the uterus; it bulges progressively more into the uterine cavity as it continues to enlarge. The decidua thus becomes divided into three parts:

1. The decidua basalis, being that part of the decidua which lies between the developing ovum and the myometrium.

2. The decidua capsularis, which covers the ovum and separates it from the uterine cavity.

3. The decidua vera, which lines the remainder of the cavity of the uterus.

The ovum usually embeds in the decidua lining the fundus of the uterus or the upper part of the anterior or posterior walls.

As the ovum continues to grow, the uterus enlarges at an even more rapid rate (see Chapter 8). When pregnancy is advanced to twelve

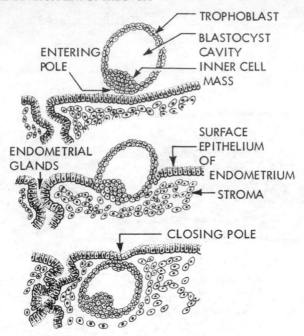

**Fig. 5/14:**   The embedding of the ovum

weeks the uterine cavity becomes obliterated by the meeting and fusion of the decidua capsularis and the decidua vera.

### Changes in the Trophoblast

While the blastocyst is becoming embedded in the decidua, a continuous process of growth and development is progressing in both the trophoblast and the inner cell mass. The trophoblastic changes must first be considered (Fig. 5/15).

As the trophoblast cells proliferate they become differentiated into three layers:

1. An outer layer known as the syncytium or the syncytiotrophoblast. Here, owing to the rapid rate of growth, the cell boundaries are not formed, and the tissue is composed of masses of small nuclei lying scattered throughout a layer of protoplasm.

2. An inner layer known as Langhans' layer or the cytotrophoblast. This is composed of single cells with complete cell membranes, known as Langhans' cells, which lie beneath the syncytium.

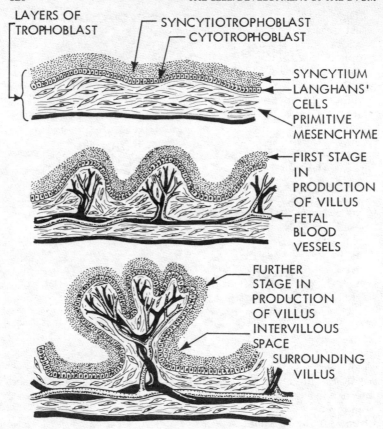

**Fig. 5/15:**   The three stages in the formation of villi from the trophoblast

3. Below the cytotrophoblast lies a layer of loose connective tissue, known as primitive mesenchyme; this is continuous with similar tissue in the inner cell mass, the point where they join being known as the body stalk.

The next changes occur in the outer syncytial layer. Vacuoles appear in this tissue, and as it thickens and increases in size these run together and form a network of little tunnels, as it were, throughout the syncytium. These spaces are known as the chorio-decidual spaces. Thus as the syncytiotrophoblast grows it invades the surrounding decidua, in the form of a network of protoplasmic meshes enveloping the entire ovum.

Digestive enzymes are being continuously excreted by the trophoblast during this time, and are responsible for the invasion of the decidua which occurs. All cells in the decidua are invaded by the trophoblast including the walls of the smaller blood vessels; when these are affected bleeding follows, and the syncytial meshwork becomes filled with circulating maternal blood. Thus the developing ovum is first nourished by the secretions of the endometrial glands, but later obtains its food and oxygen from the maternal blood which circulates through the chorio-decidual spaces.

As the process of growth continues, finger-like projections of trophoblast grow in all directions from the surface of the trophoblast into the surrounding decidua, so that the appearance of the ovum comes to resemble that of a fluffy ball. These are the primitive villi (Fig. 5/15); they contain all the three layers of the trophoblast, having an outer layer of syncytium, an inner layer of cytotrophoblast and a core of mesenchyme, and are everywhere bathed on their outer surface by the circulating maternal blood. At this stage of development the trophoblast is known as the primitive chorion.

About three weeks after fertilisation the villi begin to branch, and a single finger-like projection develops two branches, and then four and eight and so on, until a branching tree-like structure is formed. Some float freely within the maternal blood lakes, others pass deeply into the endometrium and act as anchoring villi. Whatever their size or position each villus contains the same three layers and is bathed by maternal blood. The blood filled spaces between the villi are now known as the intervillous spaces.

At this time a new system of blood vessels becomes formed in the mesenchymal cores of the villi. The vessels in each branch of the villus join together until fairly large vessels reach its base; here the vessels from adjacent villi unite and form larger vessels which pass in the primitive chorion towards the body stalk and inner cell mass. These form part of the fetal system of blood vessels. It can thus be understood that food products and oxygen, derived from the maternal blood, pass through the walls of the villi into the fetal blood vessels, which carry them through the body stalk into the inner cell mass where the fetus is developing.

During the third month of pregnancy some of the villi continue to proliferate while others atrophy. Those villi which have invaded the decidua basalis develop a very intricate complicated arborescent pattern, and form what is called the chorion frondosum. The villi in the decidua capsularis become smaller as the decidua stretches, and finally about the twelfth week of pregnancy they disappear, leaving behind a smooth layer of chorion known as the chorion laeve.

During the remaining six months of pregnancy the chorion frondosum develops into the fetal part of the placenta, and the chorion laeve becomes the chorion. Thus it will be understood that the placenta and chorion are both derived from the primitive chorion, which itself is a derivative of the trophoblast.

Stability of the placenta is not only achieved by the anchoring villi but also by decidual septa which pass into the placenta between clumps of villi and around its edge.

Under normal circumstances the villi do not invade the basal unchanged layer of decidua or the muscle of the uterine wall. Such penetration is stopped by a layer of collagen which appears between the trophoblast and decidua. This is known as the fibrinous layer of Nitabusch.

## CHANGES IN THE INNER CELL MASS

While the trophoblast is changing into the nutritional organ of the embryo, the inner cell mass is developing into the fetus, and their point of junction, the body stalk, is elongated to become the umbilical cord.

The first change which occurs in the inner cell mass is the appearance within it of two small cavities, each lined with cubical epithelium. These are the amniotic cavity, lined with ectodermal cells (which form the amnion), and the yolk sac, lined with endodermal cells. Between these cavities lie other cells known as mesodermal cells. The remaining cells of the inner cell mass are formed of primitive mesenchyme (Fig. 5/16). Thus in the region where the two cavities come closest together are situated ectoderm, endoderm and mesoderm cells. These are all formative cells from which the entire body is built up—thus all the cells necessary for the formation of the embryo are here present, and this zone between the cavities is therefore called the embryonic plate.

When the fetus is developed from the embryonic plate, the three formative layers give rise to the following structures:

*Ectoderm*—the skin, hair, nails, the nervous system, the lens of the eye and the enamel of the teeth.

*Endoderm*—the alimentary tract, liver, pancreas, lungs and thyroid gland.

*Mesoderm*—the heart, blood, blood vessels, lymphatics, bones, muscles, kidneys, ovaries or testicles.

The changes which occur during this phase of development are as follows:

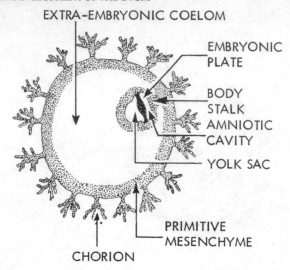

**Fig. 5/16:**  The early changes in the blastocyst

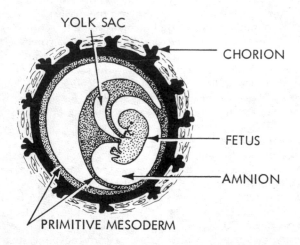

**Fig. 5/17:**  The amnion surrounds the fetus

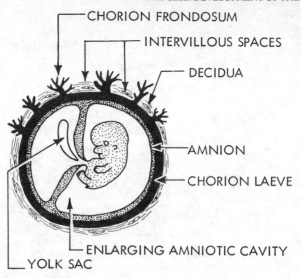

**Fig. 5/18:** The amnion undergoing expansion to line the inside of the trophoblast

## The Amnion
The amniotic cavity is filled with a fluid known as the liquor amnii. Rapid growth of the amnion occurs and the cavity becomes greatly enlarged, so much so in fact that it comes to fill the entire blastocyst (Fig. 5/17). As a result of this expansion the amnion comes to line the inside of the trophoblast, or, as it has by now become, the chorion and placenta (Fig. 5/18). This occurs much in the same way that the inner bladder of a football lines the inside of the leather casing when it is inflated. This growth of the amnion accounts for the fact that after delivery the amnion is closely adherent to the chorion and placenta.

## The Embryonic Plate
While the amnion is enlarging the cells of the embryonic plate become moulded into the form of a small fetus. The ectoderm proliferates to form the brain and the spinal cord and the skin which covers them. The mesodermal tissues grow and form the sides and front of the fetal body, and in doing so enclose between them a part of the yolk sac, which becomes incorporated inside the body of the fetus to form its alimentary tract. Later the limb buds appear and develop into the arms and legs. At a very early stage of development quite a large tail is present in the small fetus.

As the fetus is thus developing, the expansion of the amnion is in progress with the result that the fetus becomes completely enclosed by the amnion in such a way that it floats freely in the liquor amnii inside the amniotic cavity (Fig. 5/18).

**The Body Stalk**

The inner cell mass is at first attached to the trophoblast at the body stalk and is therefore relatively immobile. Through the body stalk the primitive mesenchyme lining the trophoblast becomes continuous with that in the inner cell mass.

While the expansion of the amnion and the growth of the fetus are in progress, the body stalk becomes greatly elongated and forms the umbilical cord, thereby allowing the fetus to become freely mobile within the liquor. The blood vessels which run in the body stalk from the trophoblast to the embryonic plate become converted into the umbilical arteries and vein, which pass in the umbilical cord from the placenta to the fetus.

As the expanding amnion encloses the fetus within it, it also surrounds the umbilical cord and fuses with it in such a way that the cells covering the cord and the amnion become continuous with each other.

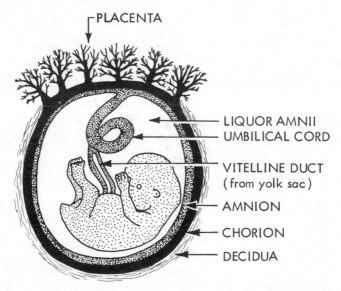

**Fig. 5/19:** The final stage—the fetus lies in the liquor amnii and the amnion completely lines the placenta and chorion

## The Yolk Sac

It has already been described how part of the yolk sac becomes enclosed by the growing body of the fetus to form its alimentary tract. The remainder of the yolk sac is caught up in the body stalk and becomes incorporated into the umbilical cord. It can be found after delivery as a small vestigial structure inside the cord which is known as the vitelline duct. Abnormalities of this process give rise to Meckel's diverticulum of the gut, which rarely may extend through the umbilicus into the proximal part of the cord.

The net result of these changes is to produce a mobile fetus, immersed in the liquor amnii (Fig. 5/19), attached to the placenta by its umbilical cord, and surrounded by two sets of membranes, the inner amnion and the outer chorion.

*Chapter Six*

# The Physiology of the Fetus

## THE GROWTH OF THE FETUS

The formation of the embryo from the embryonic plate takes place between the third and eighth weeks of pregnancy. From this time until the end of pregnancy steady growth in the fetus continues, until at term a fetus, weighing about 7lb (3 200g) and measuring 50.8cm in length is produced. The increase in size of the fetus throughout pregnancy may be seen from the following table:

| Weeks of Pregnancy | Length of fetus crown to rump (mm) | Weight (g) |
| --- | --- | --- |
| 12 | 55 | 20 |
| 16 | 100 | 120 |
| 20 | 150 | 300 |
| 24 | 200 | 635 |
| 28 | 230 | 1 220 |
| 32 | 265 | 1 700 |
| 36 | 300 | 2 240 |
| 40 | 365 | 3 250 |

Table showing the fetal growth.

It can be seen from this Table that rapid growth occurs in early pregnancy. It slows down after 20 weeks but in later pregnancy weight gain occurs due to deposition of fat in the subcutaneous tissues so that between 32 and 40 weeks the fetus 'fills out' and becomes plump.

The growth of the fetus, however, is not a uniform process. Thus at eight weeks the fetal head is almost equal in size to the body; after this time the body grows relatively more than the head, but even at term the head is much larger in proportion than it is in the child and adult.

The arms, too, at term are longer than the legs, and are not exceeded by them until the child is about two years old.

The fetal bones begin to ossify about the fifth week of intra-uterine life. The clavicles ossify first, and these are followed by the mandible, the cranial bones, vertebrae, and the long bones of the limbs.

About the fifth month of pregnancy the body of the fetus becomes covered with pale silky hairs known as lanugo; these disappear shortly before term. The scalp hairs appear about the same time and are longer and darker in colour. The sebaceous glands of the fetal skin excrete a greasy substance, known as vernix caseosa, which covers the fetus from the seventh month of pregnancy.

The erythrocytes of the blood are first formed in the villi about the third week, at which time the heart also begins to develop. The liver is a large organ during fetal life, filling the upper half of the abdomen; because of this the gut is extruded through the umbilicus into the proximal part of the cord from the fifth to the twelfth weeks. This may persist until term and give rise to a congenital umbilical hernia or exomphalos.

The sex of the fetus can be seen on inspection from the fourth month onwards. In male fetuses, the testicles descend from the abdomen through the inguinal canals into the scrotum between the seventh and ninth months of pregnancy.

At birth the infant contains about 400mg of iron, which is present partly in the haemoglobin of the red cells of the blood and partly in the liver and tissues. Red blood cells require iron when they are manufactured in the baby's bone marrow, liver and spleen, and as milk contains very little iron the baby is able to draw on the reserves in the liver and so avoids developing anaemia during the first few months of life.

The calcium content of the baby at birth is about 30g. This is utilised chiefly in the development of the bones and tooth follicles, although calcium ions are present in the blood and in all tissue fluids. Calcium occurs in combination with phosphorus in the bones and teeth, and the new-born baby contains about 18g of this substance.

Iodine is present in the thyroid gland from the sixth month of pregnancy onwards.


## BEHAVIOUR OF THE FETUS IN UTERO

Owing to the restricting space of the amniotic cavity, the fetus adopts a flexed attitude in utero, and takes up as little room as possible by bending his head and arms in front of the chest and his legs in front of the abdomen. This attitude however is not an intrinsic property of the fetus, for if there is more space available, as in cases of hydramnios, he shows no hesitation in extending his spine and limbs.

The baby functions as an independent entity after birth, and, in preparation for this, his physiological processes show marked activity during fetal life. The most important of these are as follows:

## Movements
The skeletal muscles develop about the eighth week of pregnancy and fetal movements probably begin about this time, although they are not appreciated by the mother until about the seventeenth to the twentieth weeks. Up until the thirty-sixth week the movements become progressively more and more vigorous, but after this time they are less obvious.

## Blood Circulation
The heart begins to beat about the third week of life and the fetal circulation is then set in motion. In this way adequate oxygenation and nutrition are assured when the embryo becomes too large to be nourished by the processes of direct osmosis and diffusion. The fetal heart sounds are usually not loud enough to be heard until about the twenty-fourth week of pregnancy.

## Respiration
Respiratory movements of the lungs can be made to occur by artificial stimulation of the fetus from about the twelfth week onwards. It is doubtful if these occur so early in the normal fetus, but slight breathing movements do occur normally during the last four weeks of pregnancy. These cause liquor amnii to circulate in the trachea and bronchi. During the last third of pregnancy the alveolar cells produce surfactant, a lipo-protein which lines the alveoli lowering surface tension and thereby maintaining patency of the alveoli and preventing lung collapse at birth. This is the basis of the lecithin-sphingomyelin ratio test on the amniotic fluid which is used to assess fetal lung maturity.

## Swallowing
This occurs during pregnancy, as is shown by the presence of lanugo in the fetal stomach and intestines. Radio-opaque material injected into the liquor is swallowed and may be seen in the fetal stomach on subsequent X-ray examination.

The absence of swallowing in utero is thought to be one of the causes of hydramnios, as is seen in association with anencephaly. Hydramnios occurs with oesophageal atresia, because although the liquor is swallowed, it cannot pass into the stomach and be absorbed and so regain the mother's circulation via the placenta.

## Peristalsis

Fetal gut movements are active in pregnancy as is shown by the fact that meconium, which is coloured by bile pigments, fills the bowel from the duodenum to the rectum.

## Micturition

This also is thought to be performed by the fetus during pregnancy, and to account for the urea present in the liquor amnii. In fetuses with an imperforate urethra the bladder may be distended at birth, as a result of the inability to micturate in utero. On the other hand fetal micturition is not essential, and live babies may be born at term in the complete absence of both kidneys.

## Hiccough

This also is thought to occur in utero.

One function which does not take place in utero, except in states of fetal distress, is defaecation. Under normal conditions the anal canal is closed by the tone of the anal sphincters, and no meconium escapes to discolour the liquor.

## THE LIQUOR AMNII

The liquor amnii or amniotic fluid is an alkaline turbid fluid consisting of approximately 98 per cent of water containing in solution 1 to 2 per cent of equal proportions of organic and inorganic substances. Insoluble matter and cells from fetal tissues, e.g. desquamated skin cells are also present.

In the first half of pregnancy its composition resembles that of fetal serum but in the second half it alters with decreasing sodium concentration and rising non-protein nitrogenous substances. These latter changes result from the increasing contribution made by fetal urine. Its chief constituents are:

Protein and protein derivatives
Carbohydrates
Lipids
Hormones: oestrogens rise rapidly in the last trimester
Enzymes: over 30 have been detected
Pigments: bilirubin is normally present in early pregnancy but

disappears by 36 weeks unless in the presence of Rhesus iso-immunisation

Cells: from, for example, fetal skin, amnion and umbilical cord.

## Origin of Amniotic Fluid

In early pregnancy it may be a transudate from maternal plasma, although its origin at this stage is still uncertain. Equally, transfer of water and electrolytes from the fetal circulation via fetal skin, umbilical cord and fetal surface of the placenta occurs from early pregnancy. Later in pregnancy fetal micturition increases and adds to the volume. Fetal swallowing is thought to control the volume of liquor and this may explain the presence of excessive liquor in cases of anencephaly where the swallowing reflex is absent. The explanation, however, does not appear to be quite so simple as this. The fetal respiratory tract is thought to secrete fluid which is added to the liquor but probably not to an important extent.

## Volume of Amniotic Fluid

After a slow rise to 15 weeks the volume rises steeply to 30 weeks when it levels off to 37 weeks, after which it falls abruptly. Approximately 34ml average volume is found at 10 weeks, 500 to 1 100ml at 37 to 38 weeks and 600 to 700ml at term.

## Functions of the Amniotic Fluid

The fluid protects the fetus against trauma and provides a weightless environment of constant temperature.

## Clinical Uses of Amniotic Fluid

Knowledge of the constituents of the amniotic fluid has led to the development of laboratory tests on liquor of great clinical value. These are:

1. Genetic defects: liquor can be obtained in early pregnancy and cultured so that chromosome structure can be studied.

2. Spinal defects including anencephaly: measurement of alpha-fetoprotein.

3. Measurement of bilirubin content in cases of Rhesus iso-immunisation.

4. Assessment of fetal lung maturity by measuring the lecithin-sphingomyelin ratio.

## THE FUNCTIONS OF THE PLACENTA

Study of the fetus would be incomplete without consideration of the functions of the placenta, for during pregnancy this organ does the work of the fetal lungs, alimentary tract, kidneys and certain ductless glands. Its chief functions may be grouped under the following headings:

### Respiratory Function
It is through the placenta that the fetus derives its oxygen supply from the oxygenated maternal arterial blood. Oxygen ($O_2$) is carried to the placenta in the maternal blood in the form of oxyhaemoglobin ($HbO_2$). When this blood occupies the intervillous spaces, the oxyhaemoglobin splits up or dissociates into haemoglobin and oxygen (Hb and $O_2$).

Maternal $HbO_2 \rightarrow$ Reduced maternal $Hb + O_2$

The oxygen diffuses through the walls of the villi and the reverse action takes place in the fetal blood within the villi, the oxygen combining with the reduced fetal haemoglobin to form fetal oxyhaemoglobin.

Reduced fetal $Hb + O_2 \rightarrow$ Fetal $HbO_2$

The maternal Hb returns in the mother's veins to her lungs for re-oxygenation, while the fetal $HbO_2$ is carried in the fetal circulation to the fetal tissues. Here it dissociates, gives up oxygen to the growing cells of the tissues, and the reduced fetal Hb then returns to the placenta for re-oxygenation.

The maternal blood, however, is not such a good source of supply of oxygen as is the atmospheric air, and to compensate for this the fetal blood contains more red cells, about 7 000 000 per $mm^3$, and more Hb (about 110 per cent), than are present in the mother's blood. The fetal heart action is also more rapid (about 140 beats per minute) for the same reason.

Another factor of importance is the haemoglobin of the fetus which has a slightly different chemical composition from that of the child and adult, being known as 'fetal haemoglobin' as opposed to 'adult haemoglobin'. It has the property of combining with oxygen more readily than adult haemoglobin. Curves known as dissociation curves may be constructed which show the amount of oxygen that combines with haemoglobin (this is known as its percentage saturation) under varying pressures; the increased avidity of fetal haemoglobin for oxygen is shown by its dissociation curve having a 'shift to the left' as compared to the dissociation curve of adult haemoglobin. This indicates that its percentage saturation is greater at the same oxygen tension. Fetal haemoglobin gradually becomes replaced by haemoglobin of the adult variety as pregnancy progresses, and at the time of delivery only about 80 per cent of the haemoglobin is fetal in type. At term the blood in the umbilical vein is about 50 per cent saturated with oxygen, while that in the umbilical arteries is only 15 per cent saturated.

The other respiratory function, namely the passage of carbon dioxide ($CO_2$) from the fetal blood to the maternal circulation also takes place through the walls of the villi. This occurs by simple diffusion, as $CO_2$ is much more soluble in blood than is oxygen.

## Alimentary Function

All food products pass from the maternal to the fetal blood through the walls of the villi. The process, however, is not always one of simple diffusion, and the placenta has the power, particularly during early pregnancy when the quality of the food is more important to the developing embryo than the quantity, of breaking down complex food substances into simpler compounds and then selecting those which are required. Thus proteins are first broken down to amino-acids which are then absorbed. The selectivity of the placenta is shown by the fact that the amount of amino-acids in the fetal blood always exceeds that in the maternal circulation. Some proteins, on the other hand, pass through the placenta unchanged. Examples are antibodies and agglutinins, as may be seen in cases of erythroblastosis fetalis. Toxins and antitoxins, such as those of tetanus and diphtheria, and endocrine secretions, are also readily transmitted to the fetus.

Glucose passes freely across the placenta, although the amount present in the maternal blood is always greater than that in the fetus.

The decidua and placenta contain large quantities of glycogen. This is broken down by the placenta into glucose which is then passed on to the fetus. This is sometimes known as the glycogenic function of the placenta.

Fats and related substances (lipids and cholesterol) pass the placental barrier slowly and with extreme difficulty. Some authorities consider they cannot pass, especially in the early months, as the placenta is impermeable to them; in this event the fat in the fetus is probably synthesised from carbohydrates in the fetal tissues.

The fat-soluble vitamins A, D and E are stored in the trophoblast cells and also pass through the placenta slowly; the water-soluble vitamins B and C however are transmitted readily. Sodium ions pass more easily as pregnancy advances, while calcium, phosphorus, and non-protein nitrogen are found in the fetal circulation in greater amounts than in the maternal blood. Urea, uric acid and creatinine, however, are equal in amount in both circulations and presumably pass by simple diffusion.

**Storage Function**
It has already been mentioned that the placenta stores certain food substances prior to passing them on to the fetus. Chief among these are glycogen, vitamins A and D, and iron.

**Excretory Function**
Waste metabolic substances, in addition to $CO_2$, pass by diffusion in the reverse direction from the fetal to the maternal blood, and are then excreted by the mother.

**Hormone Function**
The following hormones are elaborated in the placenta:

*Oestrogens*
The main source of oestrogens in pregnancy is the placenta but they are also produced by the maternal and fetal adrenal glands. The production of oestrogens is complex and requires close association of both placenta and fetus since the placenta lacks certain enzymes necessary to complete synthesis. This is but one example of the need, now increasingly realised, to consider fetus and placenta together as a feto-placental unit.

More than 20 oestrogens have been identified but only oestrone, oestradiol and oestriol appear to be clinically significant. Oestriol is the relatively inactive form and the placenta is capable of producing and retaining it. In pregnancy, oestriol accounts for 90 per cent of the oestrogens secreted and its measurement in maternal blood or urine is used as an index of fetal well-being.

*Progesterone*
This is produced initially by the corpus luteum and the trophoblast but later the syncytiotrophoblast takes over the entire production. It is produced in increasing quantities until immediately preceding the onset of labour. It is excreted as pregnanediol but not in sufficient quantities to make pregnanediol measurements an accurate estimate of progesterone production.

*Chorionic Gonadotrophin*
This hormone is produced by the Langhans' cells of the cytotrophoblast from the time the blastocyst begins to embed until term. It is present in maximum quantities between the sixtieth and eightieth days of pregnancy and thereafter falls to a level which remains until term. It is excreted in the urine and serves as the basis of the various

animal and agglutination pregnancy tests. Its function is to stimulate the growth and activity of the corpus luteum in early pregnancy.

## Human Chorionic Somatomammotrophin

Human chorionic somatomammotrophin (HCS) or human placental lactogen (HPL), as it is more often called, is also produced by the syncytiotrophoblast. The secretion of HPL is complementary to that of HCG and as the level of the latter falls the level of HPL rises. The hormone does not enter the fetal circulation to any extent so that all its effects are on the mother. It appears to alter the maternal metabolism so that the fetus thrives and grows and it initiates changes in preparation for breast feeding.

The measurement of HPL is also used to monitor fetal well-being in later pregnancy.

## Other Hormones

Adrenocorticotrophic hormone (ACTH), melanocyte-stimulating hormone (MSH), thyroid-stimulating hormone (TSH), relaxin (which has an effect in relaxing ligaments) and oxytocin are all increased in pregnancy. Their source, however, is more likely to be maternal and fetal rather than placental.

To a varying extent the placenta has a barrier action preventing harmful substances passing from mother to fetus. Thus the tubercle bacillus and malaria parasite are largely prevented from crossing the placenta. Viruses, being much smaller than bacteria, are able to cross the placenta easily. The rubella virus is a well known hazard if a non-immune mother is infected in the first 14 weeks of pregnancy. Infection of the fetus is almost certain with resulting congenital abnormalities such as blindness, deafness and congenital heart disease.

Drugs may also cross the placental barrier especially those of low molecular weight. Some, such as penicillin, have no adverse effect on the fetus, others such as thalidomide have a known teratogenic effect and others may produce lesser but still undesirable effect (such as pethidine, tetracycline and trimethoprim).

In general, so far as drugs are concerned, none should be used in pregnancy unless they are absolutely necessary and no drug should be used unless its safety in pregnancy has been demonstrated.

**The Fetal Circulation**

Because the fetus derives its supply of oxygen and food from the placenta, the whole of the fetal blood has to pass through this organ, while the lungs and alimentary tract, being functionless during pregnancy, require only a small blood supply. The fetus in utero therefore has a blood circulation which differs greatly from that of its post-natal life. The details of the fetal circulation are best understood by following the course pursued by the blood as it leaves the placenta, circulates through the fetus and returns to the placenta (Fig. 6/1).

The details of this circulation are as follows:

1. After being oxygenated (80 per cent saturated with oxygen) and receiving food products in the villi, the blood flows through the placenta to the umbilical cord.

2. It then passes along the cord towards the fetus, flowing through the umbilical vein. Thus oxygenated blood flows in the umbilical vein.

3. After passing through the umbilicus the vein goes to the liver where it gives off branches to the left lobe and receives the venous blood from the portal vein. Most of the oxygenated blood, mixed with some portal venous blood, then by-passes the liver through the ductus venosus to enter the inferior vena cava.

4. It passes along the inferior vena cava to the right atrium of the heart.

5. There it mixes with blood returning from the head and neck via the superior vena cava and 75 per cent of this mixed blood is diverted through an opening in the inter-atrial septum called the foramen ovale into the left atrium. 25 per cent enters the right ventricle and is pumped into the pulmonary artery and ductus arteriosus which by-passes the lungs to reach the arch of the aorta.

6. The blood from the left atrium passes into the left ventricle.

7. The blood then enters the aorta, and passes along its branches to supply the head, neck and arms.

8. After passing through the tissues of the head, neck and arms, the now de-oxygenated blood returns to the heart via the superior vena cava. The blood passes down the aorta and supplies the main body organs.

9. When the aorta divides into the common iliac arteries, only small streams pass down into the legs. The main streams of blood pass into the hypogastric arteries.

10. The hypogastric arteries arise in the pelvis from the common iliac arteries and pass up the abdominal wall, converging on each side towards the umbilicus (see Chapter 2).

11. They pass through the umbilicus and enter the cord as the two umbilical arteries. The arteries in the cord thus transport de-oxygenated blood (about 15 per cent saturated with oxygen) back to the placenta.

12. Branches of the umbilical arteries enter the villi where re-oxygenation of the impure blood takes place.

The time taken for the whole circulation to occur is about 30 seconds.

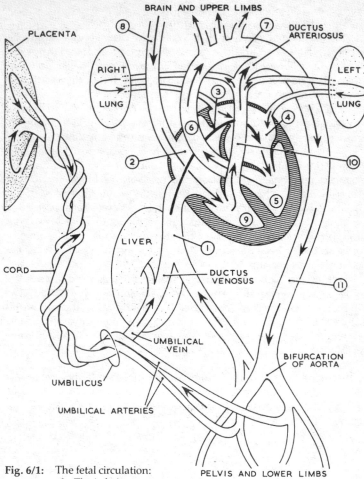

**Fig. 6/1:** The fetal circulation:
1. The inferior vena cava
2. The right atrium
3. The foramen ovale
4. The left atrium
5. The left ventricle
6. The ascending aorta
7. The aortic arch
8. The superior vena cava
9. The right ventricle
10. The pulmonary artery
11. The descending thoracic aorta

## Changes at Birth

After birth the following changes occur:

1. When the midwife clamps the cord, the circulation through the umbilical vein ceases and the vein collapses. Its abdominal portion later becomes fibrosed to form a ligament, known as the ligamentum teres, which runs from the umbilicus to the liver. It is enclosed in a fold of peritoneum known as the falciform ligament.

2. This change leads to collapse of the ductus venosus, which in its turn becomes fibrosed later to form a ligament lying in a groove or fissure in the liver and known as the ligamentum venosum.

3. With the collapse of the umbilical vein the pressure of blood in the right atrium diminishes; with the beginning of respiration and the enhanced pulmonary circulation the pressure of blood in the left atrium increases. These changes of pressure result in closure of the flap-like valve over the foramen ovale which becomes sealed off.

4. The expansion of the lungs causes blood to flow into them through the pulmonary arteries; the ductus arteriosus consequently closes and later becomes converted into a ligament known as the ligamentum arteriosum.

5. When the blood flow through the umbilical cord ceases the umbilical and hypogastric arteries contract and become closed. The latter vessels later become converted into ligaments in the pelvis and abdominal wall, known as the obliterated hypogastric arteries. The first few inches of these vessels, however, remain patent and become the internal iliac and superior vesical arteries.

In this way the adult circulation is produced, but the unwanted remains of the fetal circulation which in utero functioned as large vascular channels remain permanently present in the form of ligamentary structures.

# Chapter Seven

# The Anatomy of the Fetus

## THE ANATOMY OF THE FETUS AT TERM

The normal fetus at term weighs about seven pounds (3 200g) and measures twenty inches (50cm) in length. It has a pale pink colour, and a rounded contour due to the liberal deposition of fat in its sub-cutaneous tissues. Some lanugo may still be present on the shoulders, and the hairs of the scalp are usually dark in colour and about 2.5cm in length. The skin is covered with the greasy excretion of the sebaceous glands known as vernix caseosa, and the nails reach to the ends of the fingers and toes.

Although at term the fetus is ready to exist independently of its mother, its shape is not the same as that of a human adult, for the head is large compared to the rest of the body, and the arms are longer than the legs. The process of ossification is well advanced in the bones, that of girls being slightly ahead of that of boys. Ossification centres are usually present in the lower ends of the femora, the upper ends of the tibiae and in the cuboid bones of the feet—when seen on X-ray examination these are considered to be diagnostic of a fetus at term. The joints have a mobility greater than in later life.

The bowel is filled with meconium, a greenish-black substance with the consistency of butter. This is composed of excretions from the alimentary glands coloured with bile pigments, and contains desquamated cells from the bowel wall, and lanugo hairs from the swallowed liquor amnii.

The liver, spleen and suprarenal glands are enlarged relative to their size in the adult. In males the testicles have reached the scrotum. In females the labia majora are full and rounded due to the deposition of subcutaneous fat, the vaginal walls are well cornified and the uterus is actually larger than that of the young girl. These latter changes are due to the influence of sex hormones which have passed into the fetus from the placenta; after birth these organs regress and do not develop further until the young girl manufactures her own sex hormones at the time of puberty.

## THE FETAL SKULL AT TERM

The most important part of the fetus at term, from the midwife's point of view, is the skull. As this is both the largest and hardest part of the fetus, it gives rise to many of the difficulties which may occur during the process of birth; a knowledge therefore of the cranial anatomy is essential.

### Bones

The vault of the skull is composed of five bones, with two others entering into the formation of its lateral walls. All these bones are ossified in pre-existing membrane. They may be described as follows (Fig. 7/1):

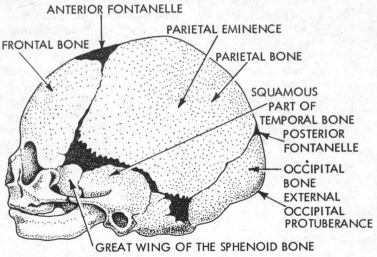

**Fig. 7/1:**    Lateral view of the fetal skull

*The two frontal bones* extend from the upper borders of the orbits to the coronal suture. They are large bones, roughly square in shape, and are curved as they cover the frontal lobes of the brain.

*The two parietal bones* lie behind the frontal bones, extending from the coronal suture in front to the lambdoid suture behind. They are the largest of the cranial bones, also roughly square in shape, and curved as they lie over the parietal lobes of the brain. In the centre of each is situated a bony eminence which is known as the parietal eminence.

*The occipital bone* is a single bone lying below the parietal bones, from which it is separated by the lambdoid suture. It is roughly triangular in shape, and covers the occipital lobes of the brain and the cerebellum. In its central part is situated a small eminence, the external occipital protuberance (or inion), commonly referred to simply as the occiput. On its internal surface is similarly placed another bony point, the internal occipital protuberance, to which folds of dura mater are attached, as described below.

In its lower part this bone forms the margins of the foramen magnum, through which the lower part of the brain and spinal cord become continuous; it also articulates with the atlas, or first cervical vertebra.

*The two temporal bones* form part of the side walls of the fetal skull. The squamous portion of the temporal bone lies below the parietal bone in front of the ear, while the mastoid portion of the same bone lies behind the ear.

*The great wings of the sphenoid bone* occupy a small area between the frontal bones in front and the squamous part of the temporal bones behind.

## Sutures

The parts of the skull where the bones lie alongside each other are known as the sutures of the skull (Figs 7/2 and 7/3). The sutures are composed of a fibrous membrane, and they allow some of the bones to overlap each other during the process of moulding at the time of birth. As ossification proceeds after birth, the bones gradually fuse together, with the result that the membranous sutures disappear and a solid bony cranium enclosing and protecting the brain is formed.

The chief sutures are as follows:

*The frontal suture* runs between the frontal bones, extending from the root of the nose (or nasion) below, to the anterior fontanelle above.

*The sagittal suture* lies between the two parietal bones and runs from the anterior fontanelle in front to the posterior fontanelle behind.

*The coronal suture* runs transversely across the head, lying between the frontal bones in front and the parietal bones behind. It enters the anterior fontanelle at its lateral angles.

*The lambdoid suture* passes obliquely across the posterior part of the skull, lying between the two parietal bones above and the occipital bone below. It passes from the mastoid part of each temporal bone upwards and inwards and joins the posterior fontanelle.

## Fontanelles

These are the areas of membrane lying between the cranial bones at the points of junction of the sutures (Figs. 7/2 and 7/3). Two are of great obstetrical importance:

*The anterior fontanelle or bregma* which is a lozenge-shaped area, lying between the two parietal and two frontal bones. It has four angles, into each of which runs a suture; thus the frontal suture enters the fontanelle anteriorly, the sagittal suture posteriorly, and the coronal suture at the two lateral angles.

It becomes smaller after birth and disappears when it is completely ossified at the age of eighteen months.

*The posterior fontanelle or lambda* which is a small triangular-shaped space lying between the two parietal bones and the occipital bone. It has three angles; into the anterior angle runs the sagittal suture, while the two parts of the lambdoid suture run into the lateral angles.

It becomes ossified when the baby is aged two months.

In addition to these large fontanelles, four small ones are present in the lateral walls of the fetal skull; two temporal fontanelles, situated at the extremities of the coronal suture and two mastoid fontanelles, placed at the terminal points of the lambdoid suture.

These have no obstetrical significance.

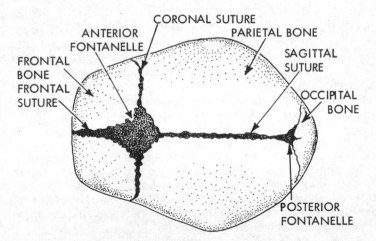

**Fig. 7/2:**  Superior view of the fetal skull

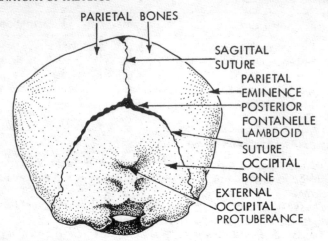

**Fig. 7/3:**   Posterior view of the fetal skull

### Regions of the Skull

The following are the regions of the skull which are of most importance:

*The vertex* is the area of the skull which lies between the anterior fontanelle in front, the posterior fontanelle behind, and the two parietal eminences laterally.

*The sinciput or brow* lies between the supra-orbital ridges below and the coronal suture and bregma above.

*The occiput* is the part of the skull lying below the lambdoid suture and posterior fontanelle. Sometimes this area is referred to as the occipital pole, and the term occiput is then restricted to the external occipital protuberance.

*The face* is the part of the skull which lies below the level of the supra-orbital ridges.

### Diameters

The presenting diameters of the fetal skull are important because they are the distances which the birth canal must stretch to allow passage of the head during delivery (Fig. 7/4). In all cases the maximum transverse diameter is the bi-parietal diameter, but the maximum antero-posterior diameter varies according to the degree of flexion or extension of the head. The maximum antero-posterior diameter thus differs according to the presentation of the fetus, as is shown in Table 1.

| Diameter | Length | Presentation |
|---|---|---|
| 1. Sub-occipito-bregmatic | 9.5cm | Flexed vertex |
| 2. Sub-occipito-frontal | 10.5cm | Partially deflexed vertex |
| 3. Occipito-frontal | 11.5cm | Deflexed vertex |
| 4. Mento-vertical | 13.0cm | Brow |
| 5. Sub-mento-bregmatic | 9.5cm | Face |

Table 1: The fetal skull diameters

*The sub-occipito-bregmatic diameter* runs from the junction of the scalp with the back of the neck (below the position of the occiput) to the bregma.

*The sub-occipito-frontal diameter* passes from the junction of the scalp with the back of the neck to the mid-point of the frontal suture.

*The occipito-frontal diameter* passes from the external occipital protuberance to the root of the nose.

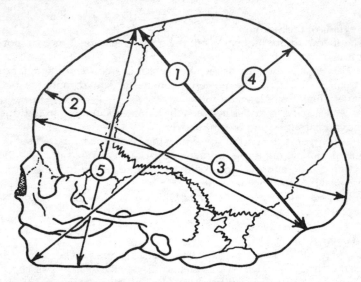

**Fig. 7/4:**   The diameters of the fetal skull   (See also Table 1)
1. Sub-occipito-bregmatic
2. Sub-occipito-frontal
3. Occipito-frontal
4. Mento-vertical
5. Sub-mento-bregmatic

*The sub-mento-bregmatic diameter* runs from the junction of the chin and the neck to the bregma.

*The mento-vertical diameter* extends from the point of the chin to the centre of the vertex. It is the longest diameter of the fetal skull.

*The sub-mento-vertical diameter* runs from the junction of the chin and the neck to the centre of the vertex and measures 11.4cm.

*The bi-parietal diameter* extends between the parietal eminences and measures 9.6cm.

*The bi-temporal diameter* runs between the two extremities of the coronal suture, and is 8cm in length.

Two further diameters of the fetus are important:

1. *The bis-acromial diameter* extends between the acromial processes of the scapulae. It is 11.5cm in length.

2. *The bi-trochanteric diameter* runs between the greater trochanters of the femora, and measures 9cm in length.

## Moulding

During the process of moulding the size of the fetal skull is reduced by overlapping of the vault bones (Fig. 7/5). Thus the edges of the frontal and occipital bones pass under the edges of the parietal bones, and the posterior parietal passes similarly under the anterior parietal. The frontal bones do not override because they are fixed at the root of the nose. In addition to these changes, the shape of the skull alters and the engaging diameters distending the birth canal become shortened. To compensate for this the diameter at right angles to the engaging diameter, lying in the axis of the pelvis, becomes correspondingly lengthened.

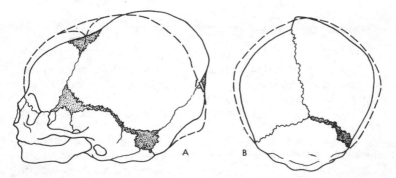

Fig. 7/5:   Moulding of the fetal skull
            A. The lateral view   B. The posterior view
            (The dotted lines show the shape before moulding)

## THE SCALP

The scalp of the fetus consists of five layers, placed in the following order (Fig. 7/6):

1. The skin.

2. A layer of subcutaneous tissue containing blood vessels and hair follicles. It is this part of the scalp which may become oedematous and form the caput succedaneum associated with difficult or prolonged labour.

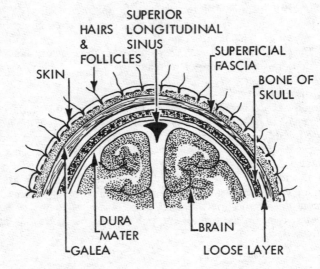

**Fig. 7/6:**   The layers of the scalp

3. A layer of tendon, covering the vertex, which connects the frontalis muscle in the sinciput with the occipitalis muscle in the occiput. This is known as the galea.

4. A loose layer of areolar tissue, which permits limited movement of the scalp to occur over the skull.

5. The pericranium. This is the periosteum of the cranial bones which covers their outer surfaces, and is adherent to their edges. Bleeding which may occur between the bone and the pericranium during labour forms a swelling known as a cephalhaematoma. This is limited in shape to that of the bone over which it lies, owing to this attachment of the pericranium to the bony edges.

## THE INTERNAL ANATOMY OF THE SKULL

In addition to the pericranium which covers the external surface of the vault bones, there is a similar membrane which lines their internal surface. Inside the skull this is composed of two layers, an outer periosteal layer which is adherent to the bones themselves and an inner meningeal layer which covers the outer surface of the brain, and is known as the dura mater. This latter membrane not only covers the whole brain but also sends fibrous partitions dipping in between the different portions of the brain, to divide up the interior of the skull into a number of compartments. The two most prominent partitions are (Fig. 7/7):

*The falx cerebri* is the line of attachment of the falx to the inside of the skull which starts at the root of the nose, follows the frontal and sagittal sutures and is continued in the midline to the internal occipital protuberance of the occipital bone. From this attachment a vertical fold of dura hangs downwards, dividing the cavity of the skull into two

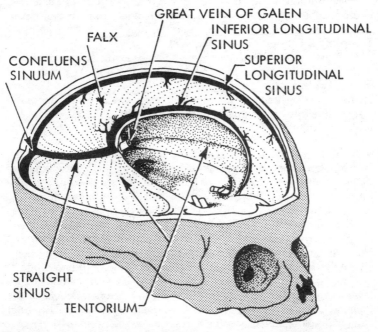

**Fig. 7/7:** The interior of the fetal skull showing the falx cerebri, the tentorium cerebelli and the venous sinuses

equal compartments each of which is occupied by a cerebral hemi-sphere. The lower edge of this fold lies free and is sickle-shaped.

*The tentorium cerebelli* is a nearly horizontal fold of dura which lies in the posterior part of the cranial cavity, forming the roof of the posterior fossa of the skull. Its line of attachment can be traced along the petrous portion of the temporal bone on each side, and is continued across the occipital bone by a horizontal line which connects the posterior ends of the temporal bones and passes through the internal occipital pro-tuberance. From this attachment the tentorium passes forwards and inwards and is attached to the clinoid processes of the sphenoid bone. It separates the two cerebral hemispheres above from the cerebellum below, over which it forms a domed tent-like covering.

The posterior part of the falx is attached to the upper surface of the tentorium along its middle line. Immediately in front of the point of junction of the falx and tentorium an arch is formed, through which the brain stem passes from the cerebral hemispheres to become con-tinuous with the medulla oblongata and the spinal cord.

These portions of the dura mater are of importance in obstetrics, because large veins or sinuses, which drain blood from the brain, pass inside them on their way to become the jugular veins of the neck. Those of chief importance are (Fig. 7/8):

*The superior longitudinal sinus,* which passes along the line of attach-ment of the falx, running from the root of the nose to the internal occipital protuberance.

*The inferior longitudinal sinus,* which runs in the lower border of the falx from before backwards, ending at the point of junction with the tentorium cerebelli.

*The straight sinus,* which is the continuation of the inferior longi-tudinal sinus which passes backwards, along the line of junction of the falx and tentorium, to unite with the posterior end of the superior longitudinal sinus. This point of junction of the sinuses opposite the internal occipital protuberance is known as the confluens sinuum or confluence of sinuses.

*The great vein of Galen,* or great internal cerebral vein, which is made up of tributaries issuing from the brain substance. It passes backwards from the surface of the brain to join the straight sinus, at the point where this becomes continuous with the inferior longitudinal sinus.

*From the confluence of sinuses the united sinuses* pass on each side of the skull along the line of attachment of the tentorium cerebelli to the occipital bone, where they are known as the lateral sinuses. They then emerge from the skull to become the internal jugular veins of the neck.

When moulding occurs at the time of delivery, the falx and tentorium and their contained sinuses are stretched. If such moulding

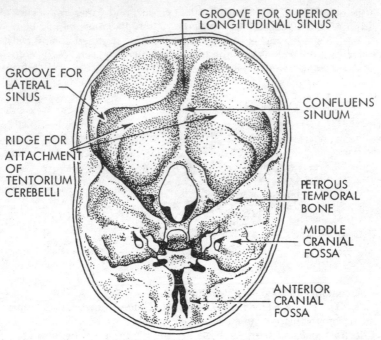

**Fig. 7/8:** The inner aspect of the occipital bone showing the grooves for the sinuses

is excessive in degree or rapid in occurrence, the membranes and the sinuses are likely to rupture; intracranial haemorrhage then occurs which may seriously affect the health of the fetus, or may even kill it outright. Such tears occur mostly in the tentorium near its attachment to the falx and are called tentorial tears. The sinuses most frequently involved in this injury are:

1. The great vein of Galen, which becomes torn off at its point of junction with the straight sinus.

2. The straight sinus, which may be involved in deep tentorial tears.

3. The inferior longitudinal sinus, which may be torn in tears affecting the falx.


## THE UMBILICAL CORD AT TERM

The umbilical cord at term measures between 15 and 120cm (average 50cm) in length, and extends normally from the centre of the placenta to the umbilicus. It is of a dull white colour, and varies in thickness from 1.25 to 1.9cm. It is composed of a jelly-like material known as Wharton's jelly, and is covered by a layer of stratified cubical cells which are continuous with the fetal epidermis at one end of the cord, and the amniotic epithelium at the other (Fig. 7/9).

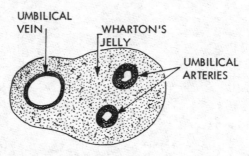

**Fig. 7/9:**   A section of the umbilical cord

It contains the following structures:

1. *One large umbilical vein*. Oxygenated blood flows through this vein from the placenta to the fetus. It contains no valves.

2. *Two umbilical arteries*. These are the continuation of the hypo-gastric arteries, which carry de-oxygenated blood from the fetus to the placenta. These wind around the vein in a clockwise manner about ten times as they pass along the cord. They have no internal elastic lamina and thick muscular walls which enable them to contract down and stop bleeding when the cord is severed after birth. This is of great importance in animals, where, of course, the cord is not ligated.

3. *The vitelline duct*. This small vestigial structure is the remains of the yolk sac. It passes through the umbilicus and in early embryonic life communicates with the gut (see Chapter 5).

4. *The allantois*. This is another small vestigial structure which passes through the umbilicus. In the early stages of development it is continuous with the urachus and the apex of the bladder; this state very rarely persists until term when the bladder opens to the exterior through the umbilicus.

The cord is not always of uniform thickness. There are sometimes present local proliferations of Wharton's jelly, which are known as false knots. On some occasions these knots may contain a loop of vessels. True knots, due to fetal movements in the liquor, are also sometimes found.

## THE PLACENTA AT TERM

When the normal placenta is inspected after delivery, it is seen to be a circular flat organ, measuring about 20cm in diameter and 62.5cm in circumference. It is about 2.5cm in thickness at the centre, and slightly thinner at the edge. It weighs approximately one-sixth of the weight of the fetus. The chorion is continuous with the placenta at its edge. It is derived from the chorion frondosum of the trophoblast.

The placenta has two surfaces:

### *The maternal surface*

This is the surface which is attached to the decidua basalis of the uterus during pregnancy (Fig. 7/10). It is deep red in colour and is divided by deep grooves or sulci into about twenty lobes which are known as cotyledons. This part of the placenta is made up of masses of arborescent villi, and the red colour is due to the blood contained in the villi and in the intervillous spaces. The actual blood vessels themselves cannot be seen on this surface by the naked eye.

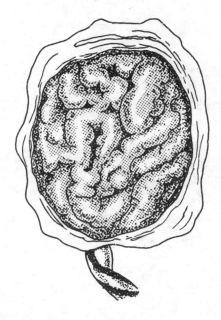

**Fig. 7/10:**   The maternal surface of the placenta

Greyish-coloured plaques may be observed attached to the surface of the cotyledons and lying between them in the sulci; these are parts of the superficial decidua, which in the sulci form decidual septa. Fibrin is often deposited on the surface of the villi, and this may in places undergo calcification which feels gritty on palpation.

## The fetal surface

This part of the placenta lies adjacent to the amniotic cavity during pregnancy, and is therefore lined by amnion and chorion which can be stripped off it as far as the insertion of the cord (Fig. 7/11). The cord is normally attached to the centre of this surface, and from its site of attachment the fetal vessels radiate out in all directions towards the edge of the placenta. The arteries and veins frequently cross each other as they pass towards the periphery, repeatedly dividing in their course, and so becoming smaller in size. They finally disappear from sight by passing deep into the substance of the placenta where they enter the villi to be distributed to all their branches.

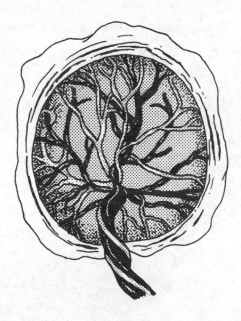

**Fig. 7/11:**   The fetal surface of the placenta

# THE CHORION AT TERM

The chorion is a rough fibrous opaque membrane which is continuous with the placenta at its edge. It lines the decidua vera of the uterine cavity to which it is loosely attached; fragments of decidua may be seen adherent to it on inspection after delivery. Its inner surface is lined by the amnion. It is originally derived from the chorion laeve of the trophoblast. At term its thickness varies between 0.2 and 0.02mm; microscopically it is found to consist of four layers of tissue, but it contains no blood vessels, lymphatics or nerves.

The chorion has little tensile strength and ruptures easily, so that retention of part or whole of the chorion within the uterus sometimes occurs after delivery of the placenta.

# THE AMNION AT TERM

The amnion is a tough shiny membrane devoid of blood vessels, lymphatics and nerves which lines the interior of the chorion and the placenta during pregnancy. It can gently be separated from these structures after delivery as far as the insertion of the cord, with the outer surface of which it becomes continuous. It consists of five distinct layers lined by non-ciliated cuboidal cells and its thickness varies from 0.02 to 0.5mm. The lining cells may be engaged in formation of liquor amnii and certainly are involved in the exchange of amniotic fluid between the maternal and fetal compartments. The amnion is much stronger than the chorion, and is retained within the uterus after delivery only infrequently.

## Chapter Eight

# Maternal Changes during Pregnancy

During the course of pregnancy marked changes take place in the anatomical structure and physiological processes of the mother. The most outstanding of these is the growth which occurs in the uterus, but practically all the systems of the body participate in changes during this time.

## THE UTERUS

### The Body of the Uterus

*Changes in Size*
As pregnancy advances the uterus grows from its normal size of 7.5cm in length, 5cm in width and 2.5cm in depth until at term it is 30cm long, 22.5cm wide and 20cm deep. The weight of the uterus also increases from 50g before pregnancy to 950g at term. During the last half of pregnancy the walls become thinner from about 13mm to 8mm.

*Changes in Shape*
In early pregnancy when the blastocyst embeds in the decidua of the upper part of the uterine body, the muscle walls of the uterus become softened and increased in length so that the cavity of the uterus is enlarged. This makes it possible for the blastocyst to increase in size during the course of its development. While the uterus is enlarging in this way, its shape becomes modified. At the beginning of pregnancy it is a pear-shaped organ; when the end of the third month is reached it becomes globular, but after the fifth month returns to a pyriform contour, which it maintains until term.

These alterations in the shape of the uterus are due to varying rates of growth which occur in its different regions. The part of the uterus first to enlarge is the upper part of the body which contains the blastocyst; it becomes uniformly enlarged and is called the upper segment of the uterus. At the same time growth occurs in the lowest part of the body of the uterus, which is known as the isthmus. As this does not normally contain the blastocyst it does not become wider, but merely increases in length, growing from about 7mm to 25mm. By the time pregnancy is advanced to two months, the enlarged upper part of the uterus is continuous with the elongated isthmus, which in its turn continues into the relatively unchanged cervix below (Fig. 8/1). The uterus thus is pear-shaped, and the empty isthmus, lying between the

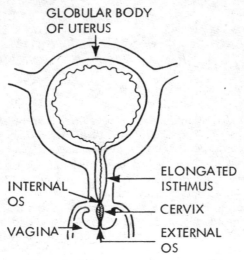

GLOBULAR BODY
OF UTERUS

ELONGATED ISTHMUS

INTERNAL OS

CERVIX

VAGINA

EXTERNAL OS

**Fig. 8/1:**    Uterus at 8th week of pregnancy

expanded upper part above and the cervix below, forms the basis of the well known Hegar's sign of pregnancy. At this stage the uterus has grown more than the developing ovum and is in consequence larger than it need be to accommodate it; this illustrates the fact that the uterine enlargement is not directly due to the presence of the blasto-cyst, but is dependent upon the hormonal stimulus of oestrogens.

When the end of the third month of pregnancy is reached the amnion expands to line the chorion and the gestation sac fills the cavity of the upper segment of the uterus. The elongated isthmus then unfolds, as it were, and receives the lower pole of the developing ovum into its cavity. The gestation sac then occupies the whole of the cavity of the body of the uterus, which in consequence becomes globular in shape.

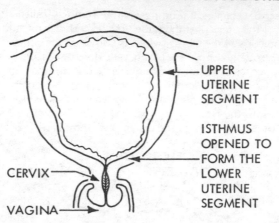

**Fig. 8/2:**    Uterus at 12th week of pregnancy

The expanded isthmus may now be referred to as the lower segment of the uterus (Fig. 8/2). The uterine body thus consists of the upper segment in its upper two-thirds, and the lower segment in its lowest third. The muscle in the lower segment is thinner than that of the upper segment, the decidua is of poorer quality, and the peritoneal covering is loosely attached anteriorly.

After the fifth month of pregnancy further increase in size occurs, chiefly in the fundus of the uterus. This restores to the uterus its pear-shaped configuration, and the insertions of the Fallopian tubes into the cornua come to lie at the junction of the upper and middle thirds of the lateral walls of the uterus (Fig. 8/3).

The division of the uterine body into upper and lower segments persists until the last month of pregnancy or the onset of labour, when the cervix becomes 'taken up' and incorporated into the lower segment. The lower segment of the uterus during pregnancy thus consists solely of the isthmus (Fig. 8/3); during labour it comprises both the isthmus and the cervix.

## Clinical Observations of the Growing Uterus
The enlargement of the uterus may be detected clinically (Fig. 8/4).

The fundus of the uterus is first palpable above the upper border of the pubic symphysis at the twelfth week of pregnancy. It reaches the umbilicus at 20 weeks and at 16 weeks is about midway between the symphysis pubis and the umbilicus. At 24 weeks the uterus is about 2 finger widths above the umbilicus.

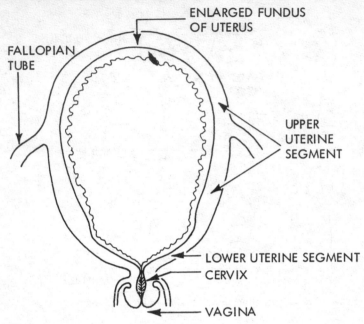

**ENLARGED FUNDUS OF UTERUS**

**FALLOPIAN TUBE**

**UPPER UTERINE SEGMENT**

**LOWER UTERINE SEGMENT**

**CERVIX**

**VAGINA**

**Fig. 8/3:**  Uterus at 30th week of pregnancy

By the thirty-sixth week, the fundus reaches the level of the xiphi-sternum gaining a point midway between this structure and the umbilicus at the thirtieth week. If these two distances be divided into thirds, the height of the fundus at the twenty-sixth and twenty-eighth weeks will be determined above the umbilicus, and at the thirty-second and thirty-fourth weeks below the xiphisternum.

After the thirty-sixth week the height of the fundus depends upon diverse factors, such as the engagement of the presenting part, the tone of the muscles of the abdominal wall and the degree of uterine obliquity.

It should be remembered that these levels are only approximations as many varying factors come into play in particular patients. Thus the umbilicus and xiphisternum vary slightly in position in individual patients, and weak abdominal muscles may allow the uterus to become anteverted instead of rising erect in the abdomen.

## Changes in the Uterine Muscle Cells

The enlargement of the body of the uterus during pregnancy is due to two factors: a process of actual growth which occurs during the first

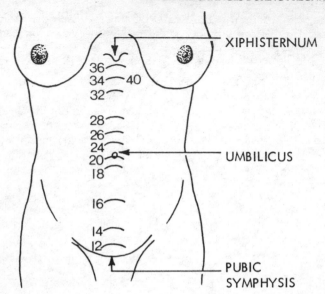

**Fig. 8/4:** The height of the fundus at different times during pregnancy

five months, and a process of stretch which takes place after this time. The muscle growth occurs in two ways; a) the actual muscle cells enlarge, increasing in length about 10 times, and in width about three times. This process is known as hypertrophy, and b) new muscle cells make their appearance and grow alongside the original muscle cells. This is called hyperplasia.

As the muscle fibres of the upper segment increase they become arranged into three layers:

*An outermost longitudinal layer,* which is continuous with the muscle fibres in the uterine ligaments. This layer begins in the anterior wall of the upper segment, passes up over the fundus and down the posterior wall. It is by the contraction and retraction of this layer of muscle that the fetus is expelled from the uterus during labour.

*A middle oblique layer,* in which the muscle fibres are arranged in a criss-cross manner. These muscle cells surround the uterine blood vessels in figure-of-eight patterns, and by their retraction after separation of the placenta during labour, they compress them and help to prevent postpartum haemorrhage. They are sometimes referred to as the living ligatures of the uterus.

*An innermost circular layer* which is the weakest of the three layers and the muscle fibres pass transversely around the uterus deep to the decidua. They are most developed around the openings of the Fallopian tubes and in the lower segment.

The wall of the lower segment is thinner than that of the upper segment and consists mostly of circular fibres.

## Other Changes in the Uterus

The normal anteversion and anteflexion of the uterus disappear after the twelfth week of pregnancy, and the uterus becomes erect as it rises in the abdomen. It often inclines to the right, producing what is known as the right obliquity of the uterus. It also rotates to the right as pregnancy advances. These changes are probably brought about by the pressure of the pelvic colon which is situated in the left side of the pelvis.

The arteries, veins and lymphatics supplying the uterus are all greatly enlarged during pregnancy. The tortuosities of the uterine arteries become straightened out as the growth of the uterus progresses.

The uterine ligaments, which contain smooth muscle, become thickened during pregnancy, as a result of the increased growth of the muscle fibres.

The changes that occur in the endometrium during pregnancy are described in Chapter 5.

### The Cervix

The cervix maintains a constant length of 2.5cm during pregnancy. However, it increases slightly in width, and becomes much softer after the third month. This is due to its increased vascularity and to the effect of oestrogen which softens the cervical connective tissue, to the relaxing effect of progesterone, to the liquefaction of the collagen, and to a great proliferation of the cervical mucosa and racemose glands. These glands excrete mucus to form a mucous plug, which occupies the cervical canal during pregnancy. It functions as a protective device and prevents the entry of harmful agents into the uterus during this time.

When examined through a speculum, the cervix is seen to have a blueish colour during pregnancy.

### The Physiology of the Uterus during Pregnancy

The function of the uterus during pregnancy is to accommodate the fetus and its appendages. In order to effect this efficiently the uterus not only has to grow and enlarge, as already described, but it must also at the same time become relaxed so that it does not expel the embryo before the time of delivery arrives.

The necessary growth occurs as a result of stimulation by oestro-genic hormones, which are derived from the corpus luteum for the first three months of pregnancy, and from the placenta for the remaining six months. In cases of extra-uterine pregnancy, marked growth of the uterine muscle occurs as a result of this oestrogenic stimulation, although the ovum is not inside the uterus.

The relaxation is brought about by progesterone, which is derived from the same sources. It also stimulates the conversion of the endo-metrium into the decidua and enables embedding of the ovum to become established.

The uterus however is not completely relaxed throughout preg-nancy. From the eighth week onwards periodic waves of contraction pass over it; they last for about a minute and recur at five to ten minute intervals. They are called the intermittent contractions of Braxton Hicks. They are usually painless and the patient is unaware of their presence. They probably have no function at this time, but are part of the physiological growth process of the uterine muscle, in preparation for the role the uterus will play during labour. Towards the end of pregnancy they become stronger and more frequent, and are respon-sible then for the taking up of the cervix when this occurs during the last month of pregnancy. When labour starts they are further increased and become true labour contractions. During pregnancy they raise the intra-uterine pressure from 7 to about 18mm Hg, which is below the pain threshold of 25mm Hg. This threshold however is exceeded when labour contractions begin and the patient then experiences discomfort or pain.

### The Vagina
The vagina grows slightly during pregnancy and develops a larger lumen. It becomes very vascular and in consequence assumes a blueish colour. These changes occur early in pregnancy and are also due to oestrogens. The superficial vaginal cells desquamate more with the result that there is an increased vaginal discharge in pregnancy.

### The Vulva
The labia minora become pigmented during pregnancy and the vulva as a whole appears blueish in colour as a result of increased vascularity. The vulval veins may become varicose.

### The Fallopian Tubes
These, along with the broad and round ligaments, hypertrophy and show an increase in vascularity during pregnancy. They are, of course, lifted out of the pelvis as the uterus grows.

**The Ovaries**

The ovaries are raised out of the pelvis as the uterus enlarges and at term come to lie just below the costal margins. As a result of stimulation by the chorionic gonadotrophin excreted by the embedding blastocyst, the corpus luteum becomes greatly enlarged during early pregnancy (see Chapter 5). At the twelfth week of pregnancy when it has reached its maximum size, it is a yellow body about 19mm in diameter containing a small cystic cavity. When seen under the microscope, its cells (luteal cells) are seen to be highly active, containing colloid particles and globules of secretion. It is known as the corpus luteum of pregnancy.

The function of the corpus luteum is to produce oestrogens and progesterone (see Chapter 4).

After the third month the corpus luteum regresses; it becomes much smaller in size, hyaline material is deposited within it and its hormonal activity is greatly reduced. The placenta now takes over its hormone-secreting function which it maintains until the end of pregnancy.

## OTHER MATERNAL CHANGES IN PREGNANCY

**Cardiovascular System**

*The Blood*

The total maternal blood volume increases during pregnancy. The plasma volume increases from 10 weeks to a maximum by about 32 weeks of 50 per cent above the normal non-pregnant volume (an increase of approximately 1 200 to 1 500ml). The red cell volume increases by 30 per cent and because this is less than the plasma volume increase the concentration of the red cells in the blood falls so that there is a reduction in the haemoglobin level. This has been called the physiological anaemia of pregnancy but this is a misleading term since the pregnant woman has a larger total haemoglobin than the non-pregnant woman.

The white blood cells also increase in pregnancy to 11–12 000 per ml and the platelets also increase.

There is an alteration in the serum protein pattern, total protein albumin and gamma globulin fall in the first quarter and then rise gradually towards term. The beta globulin and fibrinogen fractions rise and as a consequence the erythrocyte sedimentation rate rises during pregnancy up to four times its normal level.

Serum lipids, especially cholesterol, also rise.

## The Heart

Because of the increase in blood volume the cardiac output increases by 30–50 per cent in pregnancy—from about 5l/min at 10 weeks to 6.5l/min at 25 weeks. The heart rate rises by about 15 per cent.

To balance the increase in cardiac output the peripheral resistance of the blood vessels is reduced (an oestrogen and progesterone effect) so that the blood pressure remains the same.

The veins of the legs, vulva and anal canal distend during pregnancy partly due to the progesterone effect and later to the obstructing effect on the venous return produced by the growing uterus. Varicosities of these areas are commonly seen in pregnancy.

## Distribution of Blood Flow

The greatest part of the increased blood flow goes to the growing uterus where it passes into the chorio-decidual spaces surrounding the chorionic villi where an exchange of nutrients and waste products occurs before it drains into the endometrial venous system.

Blood flow to the kidneys, skin and mucous membranes also rises and the vasodilatation which results from the latter two explains why pregnant women 'feel the heat' more and sweat easily.

## The Respiratory System

Breathing remains diaphragmatic in pregnancy but with the increasing size of the uterus the movement of the diaphragm is reduced and deeper breaths are taken to increase the tidal volume. This results in an increased oxygen consumption of 20 per cent.

The pulmonary vasculature dilates under the effect of progesterone and this can be seen on a chest X-ray in pregnancy.

## The Alimentary System

Again due to the progesterone effect the intestinal musculature is relaxed giving rise to several discomforts in pregnancy. Relaxation of the cardiac sphincter leads to oesophageal reflux and heartburn is common. Gastric stasis is common and reduced motility of the intestines makes constipation a problem.

## The Renal System

The smooth muscle of the renal pelvis and ureters relaxes and dilatation occurs. This mainly involves the abdominal portion of the ureter and actual kinking of the middle portion may occur. Relaxation of the bladder musculature also takes place with the result that urinary stasis is encouraged with increased risk of urinary tract infection.

It has already been mentioned that renal blood flow increases. The glomerular secretion rate rises by 60 per cent and since tubular re-absorption remains constant the clearance of many substances is increased, e.g. urea, uric acid, glucose and amino-acids.

Conservation of sodium is maintained by a complicated mechanism whereby renin produced by the kidneys acts via a substance known as angiotensin on the adrenal glands inducing aldosterone secretion which in turn increases the resorption of sodium from the renal tubules. The maternal electrolytes are thereby maintained in balance.

In early pregnancy water excretion by the kidneys increases giving rise to frequency of micturition. This diminishes as pregnancy progresses but in later pregnancy frequency may occur as a result of pressure on the bladder by the uterus and the fetal head.

### The Skin
Increased pigmentation may occur especially involving the linea alba of the abdomen (which is then known as the linea nigra); the areola of the breasts, which become much darker; the face over both cheeks, known as the chloasma of pregnancy.

Pinkish streaks known as striae gravidarum appear in some women as pregnancy advances involving the skin of the abdomen, breasts, buttocks and upper thighs. The cause of these is as yet not fully understood and little can be done to prevent them occurring.

### Skeletal System
The bones and teeth are unchanged during normal pregnancy.

The joints show an increased range of movement especially the joints of the pelvis. To what extent this is due in humans to the production of the hormone relaxin is uncertain.

As a result of the slackening of the pelvic joints there develops pelvic instability which gives rise to the typical waddling gait of pregnant women.

### Endocrine System
Many of the endocrine glands undergo changes in pregnancy.

### The Pituitary Gland
This enlarges during pregnancy and there is evidence that the activity of adrenocorticotrophic hormone (ACTH), thyroid-stimulating hormone (TSH) and melanocyte-stimulating hormone (MSH) is increased. The production of the posterior pituitary hormones—oxytocin and anti-diuretic hormone (ADH)—is also probably increased.

## The Adrenal Glands

The medulla appears to remain unchanged in pregnancy but there is an increase in the activity of the cortex. The production of cortico-steroids rises.

## The Thyroid Gland

This enlarges in pregnancy but it is mainly due to deposition of colloid and there is no evidence of increased thyroid activity.

## The Ovaries

The function of these glands during pregnancy has been described on p. 131.

## The Placenta

This functions as an endocrine organ during pregnancy (see Chapter 6).

## Hormonal Changes during Pregnancy

These have already been discussed under placental function (p. 134).

## Changes in Metabolism

During pregnancy the mother needs a diet sufficient to provide about 2 500 calories daily. A healthy primigravida can expect to gain 12.0 to 12.5kg in pregnancy of which approximately 8.0 to 9.0 kg are gained in the last 20 weeks.

This weight gain is made up as follows:

| | |
|---|---|
| Fetal (approximately 5kg) | Fetus 3.2kg |
| | Placenta 0.7kg |
| | Liquor 0.8kg |
| Maternal (approximately 7kg) | Uterus 0.9kg |
| | Breasts 0.4kg |
| | Blood 1.2kg |
| | ECF 1.2kg |
| | Fat 4.0kg |

The average loss at delivery is 8.0kg and the average net gain 4.0kg. Obviously variations in these figures occur. Excessive weight gain in the latter part of pregnancy may indicate retention of fluid in excess of what normally happens in pregnancy and may herald the onset of pre-eclamptic toxaemia. Static weight or actual weight loss in the last trimester of pregnancy may signify failure of placental function and poor fetal growth.

## Fluid Balance

The intake and output of water are both capable of measurement, and for normal health to be maintained a balance should be kept between them. Thus water is taken by mouth, is contained in the solid food eaten, and is produced as the end product of metabolic processes in the body. The excretion of water takes place in the urine, in the faeces, by expiration from the lungs, and by perspiration from the skin. The approximate daily fluid balance may be stated to be:

| Intake | | Output | |
|---|---|---|---|
| By mouth | 1 500 | Urine | 1 500 |
| In solid food | 800 | Faeces | 100 |
| From metabolic | | Respiration | 400 |
| processes | 300 | Perspiration | 600 |
| Total | 2 600ml | | 2 600ml |

These figures are of course subject to wide variation according to the activity of the patient, the temperature of her surroundings, and many other factors.

The water balance is intimately connected with the levels of electrolytes in the blood, in the tissues, and in the cells themselves. Thus common salt, which produces sodium ions and chloride ions in the body fluids, retains water in the tissues to the extent of 1 litre for every 7 grams of salt. If it is present in excess it will cause fluid retention amounting to oedema, and so diminish the urinary output.

In some diseases, however, the fluid balance may be greatly upset, in which event the measurement of the patient's fluid intake and output and salt balance becomes important. Thus if there is an increased fluid loss by vomiting or diarrhoea the intake should be correspondingly increased either by mouth or by the parenteral route, otherwise dehydration and ketosis may follow. If the amount of salt in the body is reduced, shown by the absence of excreted chlorides in the urine, or diminished sodium and chloride ions (electrolytes) in the plasma, salt should also be given by these routes. Conversely, if the output is decreased and the intake remains unchanged, fluid will be retained in the tissues, excessive weight gain will occur and oedema may appear. This may also occur if excess salt is taken by the patient. Water, however, should not be denied an oedematous patient, for in this event there is insufficient fluid to allow the kidneys to excrete the salt already present, with the result that water is sucked out of the body cells as an alternative source of supply with consequent harmful effects.

In pregnancy considerable changes occur in fluid balance. The total water increment has been estimated as 7 litres by term of which 1.2 litres are represented by increased tissue fluid.

## Metabolism of Proteins

There is a positive retention of nitrogen in the body during pregnancy, which is necessary to build up the tissues of the fetus and the placenta, in addition to the maternal organs which enlarge during this time. About 300g of nitrogen are stored in the body between the twenty-fourth week of pregnancy and term. Marked changes are seen in the plasma proteins which are partly due to dilution effect but not entirely so. The total plasma protein concentration is reduced and the usual albumin/globulin ratio is altered from 1.5 to 1 or even less due to a fall in the albumin level.

The blood urea in pregnancy is low due to a raised urea clearance by the kidney.

## Metabolism of Carbohydrates

During pregnancy this is altered with a reduction in carbohydrate tolerance and higher concentration of blood glucose. The reason for this is complex but probably involves the effect of circulatory oestrogen, progesterone and HPL (see p. 135).

Many pregnant women excrete glucose in the urine and the commonest cause for this is a lowered renal threshold for glucose. If sugar appears in the urine of a pregnant woman on more than one occasion a full glucose tolerance test should be carried out to clarify the situation. Pregnancy may provoke the appearance of diabetes for the first time or reveal a tendency to diabetes (latent or pre-diabetes) and in either event the risk to the fetus is considerable. Knowledge of the situation allows careful monitoring of mother and fetus in the antenatal period and during delivery and improves the outcome for the fetus.

## Metabolism of Fats

The metabolism of fats occurs normally in the pregnant woman, although the amount of fat in the blood is increased during pregnancy. Fats are broken down in the tissues into ketone bodies which are used to produce energy. In the absence of sufficient carbohydrates to satisfy energy requirements, an excessive amount of ketone bodies is produced which then appear in the urine and constitute a state of ketosis. The pregnant woman develops ketosis in this way much more rapidly than does a woman who is not pregnant.

## Metabolism of Minerals

### Iron
Women are said to be constantly on the verge of anaemia mainly because of menstruation. The total haemoglobin mass contains about 2 500mg of iron and there are approximately 1 000mg held in the liver, spleen and bone marrow. Daily losses of 1 to 1.5mg occur but 10–15mg are taken in a normal diet. Only 10–15 per cent of this is absorbed into the bloodstream and in addition 10–30mg of iron are lost with each menstrual period.

In pregnancy about 500mg of iron have to be found to meet the requirements of fetus and placenta and another 180mg for blood loss at delivery in addition to 180mg for lactation. It is obvious from this that the mother's iron stores will be considerably depleted and iron supplements must be given. Folic acid, which is another factor in the manufacture of haemoglobin and in the growth of cells, is required in the same way and now all pregnant women are given combined oral iron and folic acid preparations.

If anaemia occurs either because of failure to take or to absorb oral iron then parenteral preparations can be given. Two forms are available: iron dextran (Imferon) and iron-citrate-sorbitol (Jectofer). The most frequently and conveniently used is the former given in a total dose by intravenous infusion, the dose being calculated on the mother's weight and haemoglobin level.

### Calcium
It has been estimated that the requirement of calcium in pregnancy (for fetal bones and lactation) is only 2.5 per cent of the calcium in the maternal skeleton and could be provided from that store if necessary. However, the daily allowance suggested is 1 000$\mu$g and this can be obtained from milk, fruit and vegetables.

### Phosphorus
85 per cent of this mineral is combined with calcium in bone so what has been said of calcium applies largely to phosphorus. This mineral is readily available in most foods especially milk, cheese and vegetables.

In general, what is required in pregnancy is a good mixed diet relatively high in protein (100g) and low in fat (100g) and carbohydrate (300g). This is provided by an adequate intake of meat, fish, fruit, vegetables, milk, cheese and eggs and only a limited intake of bread, potatoes, cakes and other starchy foods.

*Chapter Nine*

# The Breasts

## THE ANATOMY OF THE BREASTS

The female breasts consist of two hemispherical swellings situated in the superficial fascia of the anterior chest wall. Over the centre of each breast there is a circular area about 2.5cm in diameter, known as the areola, which is coloured pink in nulliparae and brownish in women who have borne children. In the centre of the areola is placed the nipple, a flat-topped papillary protuberance about 6mm in length.

The breast extends from the second rib above to the sixth rib below, medially it reaches the lateral margin of the sternum, while laterally it extends as far as the mid-axillary line. Its circular shape is not complete as part of the breast from the upper and outer quadrant extends up into the axilla, reaching as high as the third rib. This is known as the axillary tail.

The breast lies mainly over the pectoralis major muscle, though it partly overlaps the serratus anterior and the external oblique muscles.

The nipple of the nullipara is situated about the level of the fourth intercostal space, and is pink in colour. Its surface is perforated by 15 to 20 minute orifices which are the openings of the lactiferous tubules. Within the areola are situated about 18 sebaceous glands, which become enlarged into tubercles during pregnancy.

### Structure

The substance of the breast is composed of glandular tissue which is gathered into about 15 to 20 lobes (Fig. 9/1). These lobes radiate outwards from the areola in the manner of spokes in a wheel, and they are separated from each other within the breast, by fibrous connective tissue partitions. Each lobe is thus a complete unit and lies next to, but does not communicate with, its fellows.

Each lobe is divided by smaller partitions into numerous lobules, which are made up of masses of milk-excreting units known as alveoli. Each alveolus consists of a number of milk-forming cells surrounding a

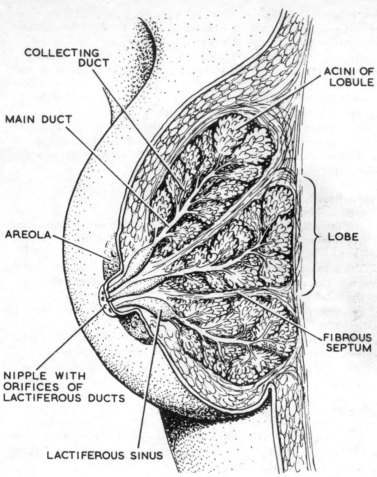

COLLECTING DUCT

MAIN DUCT

AREOLA

NIPPLE WITH ORIFICES OF LACTIFEROUS DUCTS

LACTIFEROUS SINUS

ACINI OF LOBULE

LOBE

FIBROUS SEPTUM

**Fig. 9/1:**   Dissection of the breast to show its structure

small duct into which they pour their excretion. During pregnancy this takes the form of colostrum, but after delivery it becomes changed to milk. The ducts from the alveoli join together and form larger ducts; these unite with ducts from other lobules, until finally a large duct, known as a lactiferous tubule, emerges from the entire lobe and runs towards the nipple.

While it passes beneath the areola, each lactiferous tubule expands and forms a dilated sac known as an ampulla or lactiferous sinus which serves as a reservoir for milk. From here the tubule from each lobe enters the nipple and opens independently upon its surface.

The walls of the ducts are lined by a layer of cubical cells which rest upon a basement membrane and are surrounded by a cellular connective tissue. The larger ducts near the nipple are enclosed by smooth muscle cells. The alveoli and the smaller ducts are surrounded by spider-shaped contractile cells known as myo-epithelial cells.

5. The gland is stabilised in the fat of the chest wall by numerous fibrous processes which pass from the gland tissue to the skin, areola and subcutaneous tissues, forming a fibrous investment to the whole gland. These are known as the ligaments of Astley-Cooper.

## Blood Supply
The breast is supplied with blood by:

*The internal mammary artery*, which is a branch of the subclavian artery coming from the innominate artery on the right and the aorta on the left.

*The external mammary artery*, which is derived from the lateral thoracic artery, a branch of the axillary artery which is the continuation of the subclavian artery.

*The upper intercostal arteries*, which pass along the intercostal spaces deep to the breast, coming mainly from the aorta.

The veins form a circular network around the nipple and drain to the internal mammary and axillary veins.

## Lymph Drainage
The lymph vessels form a plexus beneath the areola and between the lobes of the breast. The lymphatics of the two breasts communicate freely with each other.

The lymph drains to the following regional nodes: the axillary glands in both axillae; the glands in the anterior mediastinum, and the glands in the portal fissure of the liver.

## Nerve Supply
The functioning of the breast is controlled by hormones, and it has a poor nerve supply. Some sympathetic fibres pass to it with the blood vessels; the skin over the breast is supplied by cutaneous branches of the fourth, fifth and sixth thoracic nerves.

## Accessory Breasts
In the early fetal life of all mammals a line of immature breasts extends from the axilla to the inguinal region on each side. The majority of

these breasts disappear, the number of those persisting being related to the size of the litter the animal will later produce; in the human race all normally disappear except two which develop into the adult structures described above. Sometimes, however, small breasts and nipples persist along this line, which are known as accessory breasts and nipples. These undergo pregnancy changes and actually excrete milk during the puerperium, rarely in fact rivalling the proper breasts in size and function. Usually, however, they are small, and the patient often mistakes them for pigmented moles.

## BREAST CHANGES DURING PREGNANCY

Examination of the breasts during pregnancy reveals changes which begin about the sixth week. These are as follows (Fig. 9/2):

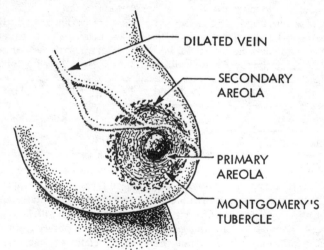

**Fig. 9/2:**   The pregnant breast

1. The structure of the breast tissue becomes changed from a soft smooth texture to one which is nodular and lumpy to the feel. This is first detected at the periphery of the breast and is due to the growth and enlargement of the duct and alveolar systems of the breast. The former is due to oestrogen influence and the latter to progesterone, in preparation for the future excretion of milk after delivery. As this growth continues during pregnancy, the whole breast gradually becomes larger in size.

2. An increased vascularity of the breast occurs. This is seen under the skin of the breasts as a network of subcutaneous veins. As pregnancy advances it becomes more intricate and widespread, until at term the veins ramify over the whole anterior aspect of the thorax.

By about the twelfth week of pregnancy further changes have occurred:

3. The nipple becomes more prominent, and the areola develops an increased fullness and pigmentation. Its pink colour changes to a brownish hue, forming the primary areola of pregnancy (see Chapter 8).

4. Some yellow bodies—about 18 in number—develop in the primary areola about this time. They are about 3mm in diameter and can be seen to contain a pin-point orifice in their centre. They are known as Montgomery's tubercles, and in structure are modified sebaceous glands. Their function is to excrete a lubricating fluid which keeps the nipple moist during pregnancy and lactation.

5. Colostrum is excreted by the alveoli from about this time, and can be expressed from the nipple if the breast is massaged from the periphery towards the centre. This is a yellowish fluid whose composition compared to that of breast milk is shown in the following Table:

|           | Protein | Fat | CHO | $H_2O$ |
|-----------|---------|-----|-----|--------|
| Colostrum | 8.6     | 2.3 | 3.2 | 85.6   |
| Milk      | 1.25    | 3.3 | 7.5 | 87.0   |

Colostrum plays an important part in the transfer of immunoglobulins to the fetus and the development of passive immunity.

6. About the twenty-fourth week of pregnancy a secondary areola sometimes appears, most often in brunettes (see Chapter 8).

These changes are physiologically the body's preparation for subsequent lactation, but they may be used clinically to diagnose the presence of pregnancy although they may be unreliable signs.


## THE PHYSIOLOGY OF THE BREASTS

The later development of the breasts begins at the time of puberty, but they cannot be said to attain full maturity until the patient becomes a lactating mother.

At puberty the breasts enlarge and assume the adult female size and shape. This is in response to stimulation by oestrogens, which reach the breasts through the blood stream from the growing Graafian follicles. Oestrogens cause a certain amount of growth of the nipple and areola, but their main function at this time is to promote growth and development of the lactiferous tubules and ducts. The breast enlargement at puberty, therefore, is due to the expansion of the duct system of the breast, under oestrogenic influence.

Non-pregnant patients sometimes complain of fullness and tinglings of the breasts before a menstrual period. This is thought to be due to congestion occurring at this time, as a result of stimulation by progesterone derived from the corpus luteum.

Further development and enlargement of the breasts next occur during pregnancy. The most important feature at this time is the hypertrophy of the alveoli in response to progesterone stimulation, preparatory to the later manufacture of milk. As the whole breast hypertrophies during pregnancy, new glandular tissue with its ducts develops, and both hormones, oestrogens and progesterone, play their respective parts in this process.

About the third day after delivery milk appears in the breasts as a result of stimulation by prolactin derived from the acidophil cells of the anterior pituitary, and they can then be said to have reached their full development.

## THE PHYSIOLOGY OF LACTATION

The process of lactation can be considered to take place in three stages:
1. The actual production of milk in the alveoli.
2. The flow of milk along the ducts to the nipple.
3. The withdrawal of milk from the nipple by the baby.

### The Production of Milk
Milk is formed as small fatty globules within the cytoplasm of the cells of the alveoli. The globules arise in the bases of these cells, and gradually unite to form small droplets. As new globules are produced the droplets are pushed towards the surface of the cell until finally they burst through the cell membrane and enter the lactiferous tubule, accompanied by a little cytoplasm of the cell substance. Here they join with droplets from other cells and the terminal portions of the tubules within the excreting alveoli become filled with milk.

Breasts which excrete milk in this way require a large blood supply and it has been calculated that milk is formed from a volume of blood about 350 times greater than that of the milk produced. The composition of milk is dependent on the metabolism of the alveolar cells, which make caseinogen from amino-acids in the blood, and lactose from glucose. The mother's diet does not affect the composition of milk, with the exception of fat, which may change its constitution if large quantities of different kinds of fat are taken in the diet.

The manufacture of milk is under the control of the hormone pro-lactin, which is derived from the anterior lobe of the pituitary gland. The action of the hormone is suppressed by oestrogens, and it is not until a few days after the expulsion of the placenta that the amount of oestrogens in the blood is sufficiently reduced to allow prolactin to exert its influence on the alveolar cells and so lead to milk production. It is then recognised clinically that 'the milk comes in' about the third day of the puerperium.

### The Flow of Milk

The milk is pushed along the ducts towards the nipple by the milk which is being continually formed behind it in the alveoli. Some of the milk is stored in the ampullae underneath the areola, until the time of the baby's next feed.

When milk is drawn off by the infant the myo-epithelial cells which surround the alveoli and smaller ducts contract and force more milk towards the nipple. This mechanism occurs as a result of a neuro-hormonal reflex. Thus the stimulus of the baby's mouth on the sen-sitive nipple reaches the brain, and by a nervous reflex a hormone is liberated from the posterior lobe of the pituitary gland. This is known to be oxytocin. It reaches the breast in the blood stream, stimulates the myo-epithelial cells to contract and causes more milk to flow to the nipple. This gives rise to a sensation, which the mother may feel in both breasts, known as 'the draught'.

The liberated oxytocin may at the same time stimulate the uterus to contract, and it is well recognised clinically that the patient may feel uterine contractions while she is feeding her baby.

### The Withdrawal of Milk

The baby sucks milk from the breasts partly by creating a vacuum in its mouth, but mainly by performing a champing action with its jaws (Fig. 9/3). Thus the baby draws the whole areola and not only the nipple into its mouth, and by closing its jaws it expresses the milk from the ampullae and then swallows it.

As the baby takes the milk from the ampullae and the lower parts of the ducts, more milk flows down from the upper parts of the ducts, propelled by the contractions of the myo-epithelial cells until the breast is emptied. The sucking reflex causes an outflow of prolactin from the anterior pituitary gland, which stimulates further milk pro-duction. In this way the breast gradually fills in preparation for the next feeding time.

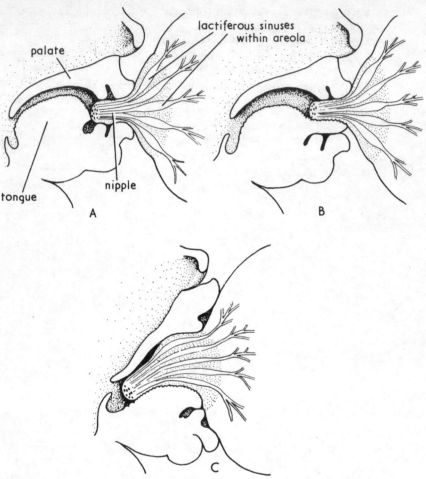

**Fig. 9/3:** The position of the nipple in the baby's mouth.
A. and B. are wrong in that the nipple is being chewed
C. is correct—the nipple is well within the baby's mouth

Thus to maintain successful lactation, the necessary requirements are:
1. An adequate intake of food and fluid by the mother.
2. Well developed breasts and nipples.

3. An adequate and frequently repeated sucking stimulus to provide the neuro-hormonal reflexes.

4. Complete emptying of the breasts.

5. A large blood supply to the breasts.

6. Ducts freed from epithelial debris.

The provision of these requirements is however outside the realm of physiology, and is part of the clinical technique of successful breast feeding.

# INDEX

*Notes*

# NOTES

# NOTES

# NOTES

**NOTES**

**NOTES**